THE SPIRITUAL LIFE

AND

THE SPIRAL WAY

EVELYN UNDERHILL

First published 2014
Copyright © 2014 Aziloth Books

All Rights Reserved. No part of this publication may be reproduced, stored in a retrieval system or transmitted in any form or by any means, electronic, mechanical, photocopying, recording, scanning or otherwise, except under the terms of the Copyright Licensing Agency Ltd, 90 Tottenham Court Road, London, W1P 0LP, UK, without the permission in writing of the Publisher. Requests to the Publisher should be via email to: info@azilothbooks.com.

Every effort has been made to contact all copyright holders. The publisher will be glad to make good in future editions any errors or omissions brought to their attention.

This publication is designed to provide authoritative and accurate information in regard to the subject matter covered. It is sold on the understanding that the Publisher is not engaged in rendering professional services.

British Library Cataloguing in Publication Data

A catalogue record for this book is available from the British Library

ISBN-13: 978-1-911405-17-7

Printed and bound in Great Britain by Lightning Source UK Ltd., 6 Precedent Drive, Rooksley, Milton Keynes MK13 8PR.

Cover Illustration: *Agnus Dei* and the symbols of the Four Evangelists. Medieval Carved Plaque (c. 14th Century)

Contents

THE SPIRITUAL LIFE

THE SPIRAL WAY

The
Spiritual Life

Preface

The four broadcast talks which are here reprinted were delivered as a sequel to a previous series by Dom Bernard Clements on the subject of Prayer. They have been revised and slightly expanded for publication; but their informal character has been retained. My object was to present some of the great truths concerning man's spiritual life in simple language; treating it, not as an intense form of other-worldliness remote from the common ways and incompatible with the common life, but rather as the heart of all real religion and therefore of vital concern to ordinary men and women. So far as possible therefore, the use of technical theological terms and direct references to Christian dogma has been avoided; but I believe all that is written here to be in complete harmony with Christian belief. The book is now published in the hope that it may be found suitable for Lenten reading; not only by those who are accustomed to religious literature, but also by some of those whom its language often puzzles and repels. I have already discussed many of the points which are here dealt with at greater length elsewhere; but those who notice this fact are asked to remember the special purpose for which these brief talks were composed.

E.U.
Advent, 1936.

Part I:

What is the Spiritual Life?

The spiritual life is a dangerously ambiguous term; indeed, it would be interesting to know what meaning any one reader at the present moment is giving to these three words. Many, I am afraid, would really be found to mean "the life of my own inside": and a further section to mean something very holy, difficult and peculiar - a sort of honours course in personal religion - to which they did not intend to aspire.

Both these kinds of individualists - the people who think of the spiritual life as something which is for themselves and about themselves, and the people who regard it as something which is not for themselves - seem to need a larger horizon, within which these interesting personal facts can be placed and seen in rather truer proportion. Any spiritual view which focuses attention on ourselves, and puts the human creature with its small ideas and adventures in the centre foreground, is dangerous till we recognise its absurdity. So at least we will try to get away from these petty notions, and make a determined effort to see our situation within that great spiritual landscape which is so much too great for our limited minds to grasp, and yet is our true inheritance, a present reality here and now, within which our real lives are now being lived. We will look at it through the wide-angle lens of disinterested worship; and put aside those useful little spectacles which bring into sharp focus our own qualities, desires, interest and difficulties, but blur everything else.

There it is, in its splendour and perfection, "shining to

saints in a perpetual bright clearness," as Thomas à Kempis said. Not only the subject matter of religion, but also the cause and goal of everything in human life that points beyond the world - great action, great music, great poetry, great art. Our attention to it, or our neglect of it, makes no difference to that world; but it makes every difference to us. For our lives are not real, not complete, until they are based on a certain conscious correspondence with it: until they become that which they are meant to be - tools and channels of the Will of God - and are included in the Kingdom of Spirits which live in, to, and for Him alone.

Christians, of course, acknowledge that Will and that Kingdom as the greatest of all realities every time they say the Lord's Prayer; that is, if they really grasp its tremendous implications, and really mean what they say. But so many Christians are like deaf people at a concert. They study the programme carefully, believe every statement made in it, speak respectfully of the quality of the music, but only really hear a phrase now and again. So they have no notion at all of the mighty symphony which fills the universe, to which our lives are destined to make their tiny contribution, and which is the self-expression of the Eternal God.

Yet there are plenty of things in our normal experience, which imply the existence of that world, that music, that life. If, for instance, we consider the fact of prayer, the almost universal impulse to seek and appeal to a power beyond ourselves, and notice the heights to which it can rise in those who give themselves to it with courage and love - the power it exerts, the heroic vocations and costly sacrifices which it supports, the transformations of character which it effects - it is a sufficiently mysterious characteristic of man. Again and again it is discredited by our popular rationalisms and naturalisms, and again and again it returns, and claims its rights within human life; even in its crudest, most naïve expressions retaining a certain life-changing power. No one who studies with sympathy, for instance, the history of religious revivals, can doubt that here, often in a grotesque and unlovely disguise, a force from beyond the world really breaks in upon the temporal order with disconcerting power.

So, too, all who are sensitive to beauty know the almost agonising sense of revelation its sudden impact brings - the abrupt disclosure of the mountain summit, the wild cherry-tree in blossom, the crowning moment of a great concerto, witnessing to another beauty beyond sense. And again, any mature person looking back on their own past life, will be forced to recognise factors in that life, which cannot be attributed to heredity, environment, opportunity, personal initiative or mere chance. The contact which proved decisive, the path unexpectedly opened, the other path closed, the thing we felt compelled to say, the letter we felt compelled to write. It is as if a hidden directive power, personal, living, free, were working through circumstances and often against our intention or desire; pressing us in a certain direction, and molding us to a certain design.

All this, of course, is quite inexplicable from the materialistic standpoint. If it is true, it implies that beneath the surface of life, which generally contents us, there are unsuspected deeps and great spiritual forces which condition and control our small lives. Some people are, or become, sensitive to the pressure of these forces. The rest of us easily ignore the evidence for this whole realm of experience, just because it is all so hidden and interior; and we are so busy responding to obvious and outward things. But no psychology which fails to take account of it can claim to be complete. When we take it seriously, it surely suggests that we are essentially spiritual as well as natural creatures; and that therefore life in its fullness, the life which shall develop and use all our capacities and fulfil all our possibilities, must involve correspondence not only with our visible and ever-changing, but also with our invisible and unchanging environment: the Spirit of all spirits, God, in whom we live and move and have our being. The significance, the greatness of humanity, consists in our ability to do this. The meaning of our life is bound up with the meaning of the universe. Even though so far the consciousness of this ability and this meaning is latent in the mass of men; yet what an enhancement of life, what devotedness, capacity for suffering and for heroism, and love, what a sure hold upon reality it already produces in those who have felt its attraction, and who respond with courage and without reserve to its demands.

When we consider our situation like that, when we lift our eyes from the crowded by-pass to the eternal hills; then, how much the personal and practical things we have to deal with are enriched. What meaning and coherence come into our scattered lives. We mostly spend those lives conjugating three verbs: to Want, to Have, and to Do. Craving, clutching, and fussing, on the material, political, social, emotional, intellectual - even on the religious - plane, we are kept in perpetual unrest: forgetting that none of these verbs have any ultimate significance, except so far as they are transcended by and included in, the fundamental verb, to Be: and that Being, not wanting, having and doing, is the essence of a spiritual life. But now, with this widening of the horizon, our personal ups and downs, desires, cravings, efforts, are seen in scale; as small and transitory spiritual facts, within a vast, abiding spiritual world, and lit by a steady spiritual light. And at once a new coherence comes into our existence, a new tranquillity and release. Like a chalet in the Alps, that homely existence gains atmosphere, dignity, significance from the greatness of the sky above it and the background of the everlasting hills.

The people of our time are helpless, distracted and rebellious, unable to interpret that which is happening, and full of apprehension about that which is to come, largely because they have lost this sure hold on the eternal; which gives to each life meaning and direction, and with meaning and direction gives steadiness. I do not mean by this a mere escape from our problems and dangers, a slinking away from the actual to enjoy the eternal. I mean an acceptance and living out of the actual, in its homeliest details and its utmost demands, in the light of the eternal; and with that peculiar sense of ultimate security which only a hold on the eternal brings. When the vivid reality which is meant by these rather abstract words is truly possessed by us, when that which is unchanging in ourselves is given its chance, and emerges from the stream of succession to recognise its true home and goal, which is God - then, though much suffering may, indeed will, remain; apprehension, confusion, instability, despair, will cease.

This, of course, is what religion is about; this adherence to God, this confident dependence on that which is unchanging. This is the more abundant life, which in its own particular language and own particular way, it calls us to live. Because it is our part in the one life of the whole universe of spirits, our share in the great drive towards Reality, the tendency of all life to seek God, Who made it for Himself, and now incites and guides it, we are already adapted to it, just as a fish is adapted to live in the sea. This view of our situation fills us with a certain awed and humble gladness. It delivers us from all niggling fuss about ourselves, prevents us from feeling self-important about our own little spiritual adventures; and yet makes them worth while as part of one great spiritual adventure.

It means, when we come down again to our own particular case, that my spiritual life is not something specialised and intense; a fenced-off devotional patch rather difficult to cultivate, and needing to be sheltered from the cold winds of the outer world. Nor is it an alternative to my outward, practical life. On the contrary, it is the very source of that quality and purpose which makes my practical life worth while. The practical life of a vast number of people is not, as a matter of fact, worth while at all. It is like an impressive fur coat with no one inside it. One sees many of these coats occupying positions of great responsibility. Hans Andersen's story of the king with no clothes told one bitter and common truth about human nature; but the story of the clothes with no king describes a situation just as common and even more pitiable.

Still less does the spiritual life mean a mere cultivation of one's own soul; poking about our interior premises with an electric torch. Even though in its earlier stages it may, and generally does, involve dealing with ourselves, and that in a drastic way, and therefore requires personal effort and personal choice, it is also intensely social; for it is a life that is shared with all other spirits, whether in the body or out of the body, to adopt St. Paul's words. You remember how Dante says that directly a soul ceases to say Mine, and says Ours, it makes the transition from the narrow, constricted, individual life to the truly free, truly personal, truly creative spiritual life; in which all are linked together in one single response to the Father of all spirits, God. Here, all interpenetrate, and all, however humble and obscure their lives may seem, can and do affect each other. Every advance made by one is made for all.

Only when we recognise all this and act on it, are we fully alive and taking our proper place in the universe of spirits; for life means the fullest possible give and take between the living creature and its environment: breathing, feeding, growing, changing. And spiritual life, which is profoundly organic, means the give and take, the willed correspondence of the little human spirit with the Infinite Spirit, here where it is; its feeding upon Him, its growth towards perfect union with Him, its response to His attraction and subtle pressure. That growth and that response may seem to us like a movement, a journey, in which by various unexpected and often unattractive paths, we are drawn almost in spite of ourselves - not as a result of our own over-anxious struggles - to the real end of our being, the place where we are ordained to be: a journey which is more like the inevitable movement of the iron filing to the great magnet that attracts it, than like the long and weary pilgrimage in the teeth of many obstacles from "this world to that which is to come." Or it may seem like a growth from the childlike, half-real existence into which we are born into a full reality.

There are countless ways in which this may happen: sometimes under conditions which seem to the world like the very frustration of life, of progress, of growth. Thus boundless initiative is chained to a sick bed and transmuted into sacrifice; the lover of beauty is sent to serve in the slum, the lover of stillness is kept on the run all day, the sudden demand to leave all comes to the one who least expects it, and through and in these apparent frustrations the life of the spirit emerges and grows. So those who imagine that they are called to contemplation because they are attracted by contemplation, when the common duties of existence steadily block this path, do well to realise that our own feelings and preferences are very poor guides when it comes to the robust realities and stern demands of the Spirit.

St. Paul did not want to be an apostle to the Gentiles. He wanted to be a clever and appreciated young Jewish scholar, and kicked against the pricks. St. Ambrose and St. Augustine did not want to be overworked and worried bishops. Nothing was farther from their intention. St. Cuthbert wanted the solitude and freedom of his hermitage on the Farne; but he did not often get there. St. Francis Xavier's preference was for an ordered life close to his beloved master, St. Ignatius. At a few hours' notice he was sent out to be the Apostle of the Indies and never returned to Europe again. Henry Martyn, the fragile and exquisite scholar, was compelled to sacrifice the intellectual life to which he was so perfectly fitted for the missionary life to which he felt he was decisively called. In all these, a power beyond themselves decided the direction of life. Yet in all we recognise not frustration, but the highest of all types of achievement. Things like this - and they are constantly happening - gradually convince us that the over-ruling reality of life is the Will and Choice of a Spirit acting not in a mechanical but in a living and personal way; and that the spiritual life of man does not consist in mere individual betterment, or assiduous attention to his own soul, but in a free and unconditional response to that Spirit's pressure and call, whatever the cost may be.

The first question here, then, is not "What is best for my soul?" nor is it even "What is most useful to humanity?" But - transcending both these limited aims - what function must this life fulfil in the great and secret economy of God? How directly and fully that principle admits us into the glorious liberty of the children of God; where we move with such ease and suppleness, because the whole is greater than any of its parts and in that whole we have forgotten ourselves.

Indeed, if God is All and His Word to us is All, that must mean that He is the reality and controlling factor of every situation, religious or secular; and that it is only for His glory and creative purpose that it exists. Therefore our favourite distinction between the spiritual life and the practical life is false. We cannot divide them. One affects the other all the time: for we are creatures of sense and of spirit, and must live an amphibious life. Christ's whole Ministry was an exhibition, first in one way and then in another, of this mysterious truth. It is through all the circumstances of existence, inward and outward, not only those which we like to label spiritual, that we are pressed to our right position and given our supernatural food. For a spiritual life is simply a life in which all that we do comes from the centre, where we are anchored in God: a life soaked through and through by a sense of His reality and claim, and self given to the great movement of His will.

Most of our conflicts and difficulties come from trying to deal with the spiritual and practical aspects of our life separately instead of realising them as parts of one whole. If our practical life is centred on our own interests, cluttered up by possessions, distracted by ambitions, passions, want - and worries, beset by a sense of our own rights and importance, or anxieties for our own future, or longings for our own success, we need not expect that our spiritual life will be a contrast to all this. The soul's house is not built on such a convenient plan: there are few soundproof partitions in it. Only when the conviction - not merely the idea - that the demand of the Spirit, however inconvenient, comes first and is first, rules the whole of it, will those objectionable noises die down which have a way of penetrating into the nicely furnished little oratory, and drowning all the quieter voices by their din.

St. John of the Cross, in a famous and beautiful poem, described the beginning of the journey of his soul to God:

> *In an obscure night*
> *Fevered by Love's anxiety*
> *O hapless, happy plight*
> *I went, none seeing me,*
> *Forth from my house, where all things*
> *quiet be*

Not many of us could say that. Yet there is no real occasion for tumult, strain, conflict, anxiety, once we have reached the living conviction that God is All. All takes place within Him. He alone matters, He alone is. Our spiritual life is His affair; because, whatever we may think to the contrary, it is really produced by His steady attraction, and our humble and self forgetful response to it. It consists in being drawn, at His pace and in His way, to the place where He wants us to be; not the place we fancied for ourselves.

Some people may seem to us to go to God by a moving staircase; where they can assist matters a bit by their own efforts, but much gets done for them and progress does not cease. Some appear to be whisked past us in a lift; whilst we find ourselves on a steep flight of stairs with a bend at the top, so that we cannot see how much farther we have to go. But none of this really matters; what matters is the conviction that all are moving towards God, and, in that journey, accompanied, supported, checked and fed by God. Since our dependence on Him is absolute, and our desire is that His Will shall be done, this great desire can gradually swallow up, neutralise all our small self-centred desires. When that happens life, inner and outer, becomes one single, various act of adoration and self-giving; one undivided response of the creature to the demand and pressure of Creative Love.

Part II:

The Spiritual Life as Communion with God

The spiritual life, then, is not a peculiar or extreme form of piety. It is, on the contrary, that full and real life for which man is made; a life that is organic and social, essentially free, yet with its own necessities and laws, just as physical life means, and depends on, constant correspondence with our physical environment, the atmosphere that surrounds and penetrates us, the energies of heat and light, whether we happen to notice it or not; so does spiritual life mean constant correspondence with our spiritual environment, whether we notice it or not. We get out of gear in either department, when this correspondence is arrested or disturbed; and if it stops altogether, we cease to live. For the most part, of course, the presence and action of the great spiritual universe surrounding us is no more noticed by us than the pressure of air on our bodies, or the action of light. Our field of attention is not wide enough for that; our spiritual senses are not sufficiently alert. Most people work so hard developing their correspondence with the visible world, that their power of corresponding with the invisible is left in a rudimentary state.

But when, for one reason or another, we begin to wake up a little bit, to lift the nose from the ground and notice that spiritual light and that spiritual atmosphere as real constituents of our human world; then, the whole situation is changed. Our horizon is widened, our experience is enormously enriched, and at the same time our responsibilities are enlarged. For now we get an entirely new idea of what human beings are for, and what they can achieve: and as a result, first our notions about life, our scale of values, begins to change, and then we do.

Here the creative action of God on a human creature enters on a new phase; for the mysterious word creation does not mean a routine product, neatly finished off and put on a shelf. Mass-production is not creation. Thus we do not speak of the creation of a pot of jam; though we might speak of the creation of a salad, for there freedom and choice play a major part. No two salads are ever quite alike. Creation is the activity of an artist possessed by the vision of perfection; who, by means of the raw material with which he works, tries to give more and more perfect expression to his idea, his inspiration or his love. From this point of view, each human spirit is an unfinished product, on which the Creative Spirit is always at work.

The moment in which, in one way or another, we become aware of this creative action of God and are therefore able to respond or resist, is the moment in which our conscious spiritual life begins. In all the talk of human progress, it is strange how very seldom we hear anything about this, the most momentous step forward that a human being can make: for it is the step that takes us beyond self-interest, beyond succession, sets up a direct intercourse with the soul's Home and Father, and can introduce us into eternal life. Large parts of the New Testament are concerned with the making of that step. But the experimental knowledge of it is not on the one hand possessed by all Christians, nor on the other hand is it confined to Christianity.

There are many different ways in which the step can be taken. It may be, from the ordinary human point of view, almost imperceptible: because, though it really involves the very essence of man's being, his free and living will, it is not linked with a special or vivid experience. Bit by bit the inexorable pressure is applied, and bit by bit the soul responds; until a moment comes when it realises that the landscape has been transformed, and is seen in anew proportion and lit by a new light. So the modern French woman whose memoirs were published under the name of Lucie Christine was not conscious of any jolt or dislocation of her life, but only of a disclosure of its true meaning and direction, on the day when she seemed to see before her eyes the words "God Only!" and received from them an over-whelming conviction of His reality which enlightened her mind, attracted her heart and gave power to her will. Yet this was really the gentle, long prepared initiation of her conscious spiritual life.

But sometimes the steps is a distinct and vivid experience. Then we get the strange facts of conversion: when through some object or event - perhaps quite small object or event - in the external world, another world and its overwhelming attraction and demand is realised. An old and limited state of consciousness is suddenly, even violently, broken up and another takes its place. It was the voice of a child saying "Take, read!" which at last made St. Augustine cross the frontier on which he had been lingering, and turned a brilliant and selfish young professor into one of the giants of the Christian Church; and a voice which seemed to him to come from the Crucifix, which literally made the young St. Francis, unsettled and unsatisfied, another man than he was before. It was while St. Ignatius sat by a stream and watched the running water, and while the strange old cobbler Jacob Boehme was looking at the pewter dish, that there was shown to each of them the mystery of the Nature of God. It was the sudden sight of a picture at a crucial moment of her life which revealed to St. Catherine of Genoa the beauty of Holiness, and by contrast her own horribleness; and made her for the rest of her life the friend and servant of the unseen Love. All these were various glimpses of one living Perfection; and woke up the love and desire for that living perfection, latent in every human creature, which is the same thing as the love of God, and the substance of a spiritual life. A spring is touched, a Reality always there discloses itself in its awe-inspiring majesty and intimate nearness, and becomes the ruling fact of existence; continually presenting its standards, and demanding a costly response. And so we get such an astonishing scene, when we reflect upon it, as that of the young Francis of Assisi, little more than a boy, asking all night long the one question which so many apparently mature persons have never asked at all: "My God and All, what art Thou and what am I?" and we realise with amazement what a human creature really is - a finite centre of consciousness, which is able to apprehend, and long for, Infinity.

In all the records of those who have had this experience, we notice that there is always the sense that we are concerned with two realities, not one: that while it is true that there is something in man which longs for the Perfect and can move towards it, what matters most and takes precedence of all else is the fact of a living Reality over against men, who stoops toward him, and first incites and then supports and responds to his seeking. And it is through this strange communion between the finite and the Infinite, the seeker and the sought, the creature man and the Creator God - which we may sometimes think of in impersonal terms borrowed from physical nature and sometimes in personal terms borrowed from the language of human love - that the spiritual life develops in depth and power.

Of course, in all this we are trying to think and speak of

things which lie at the outer fringe of our consciousness, and of which at best our perception must be dim; for they are almost out of focus, though we know that they are there. So, while we must avoid too much indefiniteness and abstraction on one hand, we must also avoid hard and fast definitions on the other hand. For no words in our human language are adequate or accurate when applied to spiritual realities; and it is the saints and not the sceptics who have most insisted on this. "No knowledge of God which we get in this life is true knowledge," says St. John of the Cross. It is always confused, imperfect, oblique. Were it otherwise, it would not be knowledge of God. But we are helped by the fact that all the responses of men to the incitement of this hidden God, however it may reach them, follow much the same road; even though they may call its various stages by very different names. All mean on one hand action, effort, renunciation of the narrow horizon, the personal ambition, the unreal objective; and on the other hand a deliberate and grateful response to the attraction of the unseen, deepening into a conscious communion which gradually becomes the ruling fact of life.

The old writers call these two activities Mortification and Prayer. These are formidable words, and modern man tends to recoil from them. Yet they only mean, when translated into our own language, that the development of the spiritual life involves both dealing with ourselves, and attending to God. Or, to put it the other way round and in more general terms, first turning to Reality, and then getting our tangled, half-real psychic lives - so tightly coiled about ourselves and our own interests, including our spiritual interests - into harmony with the great movement of Reality. Mortification means killing the very roots of self-love; pride and possessiveness, anger and violence, ambition and greed in all their disguises, however respectable those disguises may be, whatever uniforms they wear. In fact, it really means the entire transformation of our personal, professional and political life into something more consistent with our real situation as small dependent, fugitive creatures; all sharing the same limitations and inheriting the same half-animal past. That may not sound very impressive or unusual; but it is the foundation of all genuine spiritual life, and sets a standard which is not peculiar to orthodox Christianity. Those who are familiar with Blake's poetry will recognise that it is all to be found there. Indeed, wherever we find people whose spiritual life is robust and creative, we find that in one way or another this transformation has been effected and this price has been paid.

Prayer means turning to Reality, taking our part, however humble, tentative and half-understood, in the continual conversation, the communion, of our spirits with the Eternal Spirit; the acknowledgment of our entire dependence, which is yet the partly free dependence of the child. For Prayer is really our whole life toward God: our longing for Him, our "incurable God-sickness," as Barth calls it, our whole drive towards Him. It is the humble correspondence of the human spirit with the Sum of all Perfection, the Fountain of Life. No narrower definition than this is truly satisfactory, or covers all the ground. Here we are, small half-real creatures of sense and spirit, haunted by the sense of a Perfection ever calling to us, and yet ourselves so fundamentally imperfect, so hopelessly involved in an imperfect world; with a passionate desire for beauty, and more mysteriously still, a knowledge of beauty, and yet unable here to realise perfect beauty; with a craving for truth and a deep reverence for truth, but only able to receive flashes of truth. Yet we know that perfect goodness, perfect beauty, and perfect truth exist within the Life of God; and that our hearts will never rest in less than these. This longing, this need of God, however dimly and vaguely we feel it, is the seed from which grows the strong, beautiful and fruitful plant of prayer. It is the first response of our deepest selves to the attraction of the Perfect; the recognition that He has made us for Himself, that we depend on Him and are meant to depend on Him, and that we shall not know the meaning of peace until our communion with Him is at the centre of our lives.

"Without Thee, I cannot live!" Whatever our small practice, belief, or experience may be, nothing can alter the plain fact that God, the Spirit of spirits, the Life-giving Life, has made or rather is making each person reading these words for Himself, and that our lives will not achieve stability until they are ruled by that truth. All creation has purpose. It looks towards perfection. "In the volume of the book it is written of me, that I should fulfil thy will, O God." Not in some mysterious spiritual world that I know nothing about; but here and now, where I find myself, as a human creature of spirit and of sense, immersed in the modern world - subject to time with all its vicissitudes, and yet penetrated by the Eternal, and finding reality not in one but in both. To acknowledge and take up that double obligation to the seen and the unseen, in however homely and practical a way, is to enter consciously upon the spiritual life. That will mean time and attention given to it; a deliberate drawing-in from the circumference to the centre, that "setting of life in order" for which St. Thomas Aquinas prayed.

One of the great French teachers of the seventeenth century, Cardinal de Bérulle, summed up the relation of man to God in three words: Adoration, Adherence, Co-operation. This means, that from first to last the emphasis is to be on God and not on ourselves. Admiring delight, not cadging demands. Faithful and childlike dependence - a clinging to the Invisible, as the most real of all realities, in all the vicissitudes of life - not mere self-expression and self-fulfilment. Disinterested collaboration in the Whole, in God's vast plan and purpose; not concentration on our own small affairs. Three kinds of generosity. Three kinds of self-forgetfulness. There we have the formula of the spiritual life: a confident reliance on the immense fact of His Presence, everywhere and at all times, pressing on the soul and the world by all sorts of paths and in all sorts of ways, pouring out on it His undivided love, and demanding an undivided loyalty. The discovery that this is happening all the time, to the just and the unjust - and that we are simply being invited to adore and to serve that which is already there - once it has become a living conviction for us, will inevitably give to our spiritual life a special quality of gratitude, realism, trust. We stand in a world completely penetrated by the Living God, the abiding Source and Sum of Reality. We are citizens of that world now; and our whole life is or should be an acknowledgment of this.

"If I climb up into heaven, thou art there: if I go down to hell, thou art there also. If I take the wings of the morning; and remain in the uttermost parts of the sea; even there also shall thy hand lead me; and thy right hand shall hold me."

Consider for a moment what, in practice, the word Adoration implies. The upward and outward look of humble and joyful admiration. Awe-struck delight in the splendour and beauty of God, the action of God and Being of God, in and for Himself alone, as the very colour of life: giving its quality of unearthly beauty to the harshest, most disconcerting forms and the dreariest stretches of experience. This is adoration: not a difficult religious exercise, but an attitude of the soul. "To thee I lift up mine eyes, O thou that dwellest in the heavens": I don't turn round and look at myself. Adoration begins to purify us from egotism straight away. It may not always be easy - in fact, for many people it is not at all easy - but it is realism; the atmosphere within which alone the spiritual life can be lived. Our Father which art in heaven, hallowed be Thy Name! That tremendous declaration, with its unlimited confidence and unlimited awe, governs everything else.

What a contrast this almost inarticulate act of measureless adoration is, to what Karl Barth calls the dreadful prattle of theology. Hallowed be thy Name: not described: or analysed be thy Name. Before that Name, let the most soaring intellects cover their eyes with their wings, and adore. Compared with this, even the coming of the Kingdom and the doing of the Will are side issues; particular demonstrations of the Majesty of the Infinite God, on whom all centres, and for whom all is done. People who are apt to say that adoration is difficult and it is so much easier to pray for practical things, might remember that in making this great act of adoration they are praying for extremely practical things: among others, that their own characters, homes, social contacts, work, conversation, amusements and politics may be cleansed from imperfection, sanctified. For all these are part of God's Universe; and His Name must be hallowed in and through them, if they are to be woven into the Divine world, and made what they were meant to be.

A spiritual life involves the setting of our will towards all this. The Kingdom must come as a concrete reality, with a power that leaves no dark corners outside its radius; and the

Will be done in this imperfect world, as it is in the perfect world of Eternity. What really seems to you to matter most? The perfection of His mighty symphony, or your own remarkably clever performance of that difficult passage for the tenth violin? And again, if the music unexpectedly requires your entire silence, which takes priority in your feelings? The mystery and beauty of God's orchestration? Or the snub administered to you? Adoration, widening our horizons, drowning our limited interests in the total interests of Reality, redeems the spiritual life from all religious pettiness, and gives it a wonderful richness, meaning and span. And more, every aspect, even the most homely, of our practical life can become part of this adoring response, this total life; and always has done in those who have achieved full spiritual personality. "All the earth doth worship thee" means what it says. The life, beauty and meaning of the whole created order, from the tomtit to the Milky Way, refers back to the Absolute Life and Beauty of its Creator: and so perceived, so lived, every bit has spiritual significance. Thus the old woman of the legend could boil her potatoes to the greater glory of God; and St. Teresa, taking her turn in the kitchen, found Him very easily among the pots and pans.

So here we get, balancing and completing each other, the two first conditions which are to govern man's conscious spiritual life. First, the unspeakable perfection, beauty and attraction of God, absolute in His independent splendour, and calling forth our self-oblivious adoration. And next, the fact that this same infinite God, everywhere present, pours out His undivided love on each of His creatures, and calls each into an ever deepening communion with Him, a more complete and confident adherence. The completeness of the Perfect includes a completeness of self-giving which yet leaves His essential Being undiminished and unexpressed. He rides upon the floods. It is because of our own limitations that we seem only to receive Him in the trickles. Thus an attitude of humble and grateful acceptance, a self-opening, an expectant waiting, comes next to adoration as the second essential point in the development of the spiritual life. In that life, the spiritually hungry are always filled, if not always with the precise kind of food they expected; and the spiritually rich are sent empty away.

That, of course, is the moral of the story of the Publican and the Pharisee. The Publican's desperate sense of need and imperfection made instant contact with the source of all perfection. He stood afar off, saying "God be merciful, be generous, to me a sinner!" He had got the thing in proportion. We need not suppose that he was a specially wicked man; but he knew he was an imperfect, dependent, needy man, without any claims or any rights. He was a realist. That opened a channel, and started a communion, between the rich God and the poor soul. But the Pharisee's accurate statement of his own excellent situation made no contact with the realities of the Spirit, started no communion. He was dressed in his own spiritual self-esteem; and it acted like a mackintosh. The dew of grace could not get through. "I thank thee, Lord, that I am a good Churchman, a good patriot, a good neighbour." Along those lines there is absolutely nothing doing. No communion between spirit and spirit. No adherence to reality. Osuna says that God plays a game with the soul called "the loser wins"; a game in which the one who holds the poorest cards does best. The Pharisee's consciousness that he had such an excellent hand really prevented him from taking a single trick.

Part III:

The Spiritual Life as Cooperation with God

We come now to the last of Bérulle's three ingredients of a spiritual life: Co-operation. What does that mean? It means that we shall not live up to our call as spiritual creatures unless we are willing to pull our weight. The theological axiom that "Man's will and God's grace rise and fall together" must be translated into practical terms, and given practical effect. More is required of those who wake up to reality, than the passive adoration of God or intimate communion with God. Those responses, great as they are, do not cover the purpose of our creation. The riches and beauty of the spiritual landscape are not disclosed to us in order that we may sit in the sun parlour, be grateful for the excellent hospitality, and contemplate the glorious view. Some people suppose that the spiritual life mainly consists in doing that. God provides the spectacle. We gaze with reverent appreciation from our comfortable seats, and call this proceeding Worship.

No idea of our situation could be more mistaken than this. Our place is not the auditorium but the stage - or, as the case may be, the field, workshop, study, laboratory - because we ourselves form part of the creative apparatus of God, or at least are meant to form part of the creative apparatus of God. He made us in order to use us, and use us in the most profitable way; for His purpose, not ours. To live a spiritual life means subordinating all other interests to that single fact. Sometimes our positions seems to be that of tools; taken up when wanted, used in ways which we had not expected for an object on which our opinion is not asked, and then laid down. Sometimes we are the currency used in some great operation, of which the purpose is not revealed to us. Sometimes we are servants, left year in, year out to the same monotonous job. Sometimes we are conscious fellow-workers with the Perfect, striving to bring the Kingdom in. But whatever our particular place or job may be, it means the austere conditions of the workshop, not the free-lance activities of the messy but well-meaning amateur; clocking in at the right time and tending the machine in the right way. Sometimes, perhaps, carrying on for years with a machine we do not very well understand and do not enjoy; because it needs doing, and no one else is available. Or accepting the situation quite quietly, when a job we felt that we were managing excellently is taken away. Taking responsibility if we are called to it, or just bringing the workers their dinner, cleaning and sharpening the tools. All self-willed choices and obstinacy drained out of what we thought to be our work; so that it becomes more and more God's work in us.

I go back to the one perfect summary of man's Godward life and call - the Lord's Prayer. Consider how dynamic and purposive is its character. Thy Will be done - Thy Kingdom come! There is energy, drive, purpose in those words; an intensity of desire for the coming of perfection into life. Not the limp resignation that lies devoutly in the road and waits for the steam roller; but a total concentration on the total interests of God, which must be expressed in action. It is useless to utter fervent petitions for that Kingdom to be established and that Will be done, unless we are willing to do something about it ourselves. As we walk through London we know very well that we are not walking through the capital of the Kingdom of Heaven. Yet we might be, if the conviction and action of every

Christian in London were set without any conditions or any reluctance towards this end; if there were perfect consistency, whatever it cost - and it is certain that the cost would not be small - between our spiritual ideals and our social and political acts.

We are the agents of the Creative Spirit, in this world. Real advance in the spiritual life, then, means accepting this vocation with all it involves. Not merely turning over the pages of an engineering magazine and enjoying the pictures, but putting on overalls and getting on with the job. The real spiritual life must be horizontal as well as vertical; spread more and more as well as aspire more and more. It must be larger, fuller, richer, more generous in its interests than the natural life alone can ever be; must invade and transform all homely activities and practical things. For it means an offering of life to the Father of life, to Whom it belongs; a willingness - an eager willingness - to take our small place in the vast operations of His Spirit, instead of trying to run a poky little business on our own.

So now we come back to this ordinary mixed life of every day, in which we find ourselves - the life of house and work, tube and aeroplane, newspaper and cinema, wireless and television, with its tangle of problems and suggestions and demands - and consider what we are to do about that; how, within its homely limitations, we can cooperate with the Will. It is far easier, though not very easy, to develop and preserve a spiritual outlook on life, than it is to make our everyday actions harmonise with that spiritual outlook. That means trying to see things, persons and choices from the angle of eternity; and dealing with them as part of the material in which the Spirit works. This will be decisive for the way we behave as to our personal, social, and national obligations. It will decide the papers we read, the movements we support, the kind of administrators we vote for, our attitude to social and international justice. For though we may renounce the world for ourselves, refuse the attempt to get anything out of it, we have to accept it as the sphere in which we are to cooperate with the Spirit, and try to do the Will. Therefore the prevalent notion that spirituality and politics have nothing to do with one another is the exact opposite of the truth. Once it is accepted in a realistic sense, the Spiritual Life has everything to do with politics. It means that certain convictions about God and the world become the moral and spiritual imperatives of our life; and this must be decisive for the way we choose to behave about that bit of the world over which we have been given a limited control.

The life of this planet, and especially its human life, is a life in which something has gone wrong, and badly wrong. Every time that we see an unhappy face, an unhealthy body, hear a bitter or despairing word, we are reminded of that. The occasional dazzling flashes of pure beauty, pure goodness, pure love which show us what God wants and what He is, only throw into more vivid relief the horror of cruelty, greed, oppression, hatred, ugliness; and also the mere muddle and stupidity which frustrate and bring suffering into life. Unless we put on blinkers, we can hardly avoid seeing all this; and unless we are warmly wrapped up in our own cosy ideas, and absorbed in our own interests, we surely cannot help feeling the sense of obligation, the shame of acquiescence, the call to do something about it. To say day by day "Thy Kingdom Come" - if these tremendous words really stand for a conviction and desire - does not mean "I quite hope that some day the Kingdom of God will be established, and peace and goodwill prevail. But at present I don't see how it is to be managed or what I can do about it." On the contrary, it means, or should mean, "Here am I! Send me!" - active, costly collaboration with the Spirit in whom we believe.

Consider the story of the call of the young Isaiah. It is a story so well known that we easily take it for granted, and so fail to realise it as one of the most magnificent and significant in the world; for it shows us the awakening of a human being to his true situation over against Reality, and the true object of his fugitive life. There are three stages in it. First, the sudden disclosure of the Divine Splendour; the mysterious and daunting beauty of Holiness, on which even the seraphs dare not look. The veil is lifted, and the Reality which is always there is revealed. And at once the young man sees, by contrast, his own dreadful imperfection. "Woe is me! for I am a man of unclean lips!" The vision of perfection, if it is genuine, always brings shame, penitence, and therefore purification. That is the second stage. What is the third? The faulty human creature, who yet possesses the amazing power of saying Yes or No to the Eternal God, is asked for his services, and instantly responds. "Who will go for us?" "Here am I! send me!" There the very essence of the spiritual life is gathered and presented in a point: first the vision of the Perfect, and the sense of imperfection and unworthiness over against the Perfect, and then because of the vision, and in spite of the imperfection, action in the interests of the Perfect - co-operation with God.

The action may be almost anything; from the ceaseless self-offering of the enclosed nun to the creation of beauty, or the clearance of slums. "Here am I! send me!" means going anyhow, anywhere, at any time. Not where the prospects are good, but where the need is great; not to the obviously suitable job, which I'm sure that I can do with distinction; but to do the difficult thing, or give the unpopular message, in the uncongenial place. "And Moses said, Who am I, that I should go to Pharaoh and bring forth the children of Israel out of Egypt?" But he did it. Indeed, it is a peculiarity of the great spiritual personality that he or she constantly does in the teeth of circumstances what other people say cannot be done. He is driven by a total devotion which overcomes all personal timidity, and gives a power unknown to those who are playing for their own hand or carving their own career.

If we consider the lives of the Saints, we see the strange paths along which they were driven by the Will to the accomplishment of their destiny: how unexpected and uncongenial were the ways in which they were used to bring the Kingdom in and do the Will of God: and how the heavenly Bread which they were given was given to make them strong for this destiny, not because it tasted nice. Great courage and initiative, the hardy endurance of privation and fatigue, the calm acceptance of unpopularity, misunderstanding and contempt, are at least as characteristic of them as any of the outward marks of piety. So too their inner life, which we are inclined to think of as a constant succession of spiritual delights, was often hard and painful. Willingly and perpetually, they prayed from within the Cross, shared the agony, darkness, loneliness of the Cross; and because of this, they shared in its saving power.

The Church is in the world to save the world. It is a tool of God for that purpose; not a comfortable religious club established in fine historical premises. Every one of its members is required, in one way or another, to co-operate with the Spirit in working for that great end: and much of this work will be done in secret and invisible ways. We are transmitters as well as receivers. Our contemplation and our action, our humble self-opening to God, keeping ourselves sensitive to His music and light, and our generous self opening to our fellow creatures, keeping ourselves sensitive to their needs, ought to form one life; meditating between God and His world, and bringing the saving power of the Eternal into time. We are far from realising all that human spirits can do for one another on spiritual levels if they will pay the price; how truly and really our souls interpenetrate, and how impossible and un-Christian it is to "keep ourselves to ourselves." When St. Catherine of Siena used to say to the sinners who came to her: "Have no fear, I will take the burden of your sins," she made a practical promise, which she fulfilled literally and at her own great cost. She could do this because she was totally self-given to the purposes of the Spirit, was possessed by the Divine passion of saving love, and so had taken her place in the great army of rescuing souls.

That army continues in being, and the call to serve in its ranks would be more frequent and effective if we believed in it a little more: believed in it so much that we were willing to give time and strength to it, and did not draw back when we found that we had to suffer for it. "You will never do much for people, except by suffering for them," said the Abbé Huvelin. In the world of the Spirit that is supremely true. Again and again in the saints we see this saving action of love; but never apart from pain and self-oblation. Real intercession is a form of sacrifice; and sacrifice always costs something, always means suffering, even though the most deeply satisfying joy of which we are capable is mingled with its pain. The thoughts of God are very deep. Bit by bit He moulds us to His image, by giving to us some of His saving power, His redemptive love, and asking our co-operation. From time to time it is our privilege to meet these redemptive souls. They are always people, of course, who love God much, and - as St. Thomas says about Charity - love other people with the same love as that with which they love God; a love which is not satisfied unless it is expressed in sacrifice. When they find someone struggling with temptation, or persisting in wrong-doing, or placed in great spiritual danger, they are moved to a passionate and unconditional self-offering on that person's behalf. If the offering is accepted and the prayer is effective, it means much suffering for the redeeming soul; and presently it appears that the situation has been changed, the temptation has been mastered, the wrongdoing has ceased. When we find ourselves in the presence of such facts as these we are awed and silenced; and our own petty notions of what the spiritual life of man may be and do are purified and enlarged. Cause and effect, perhaps, may not be visible on the surface. But below the surface, there has been a costly victory of love.

We come down from these heights to consider what this complete self-giving to the Spirit can mean in our own quite ordinary lives. St. John of the Cross says that every quality or virtue which that Spirit really produces in men's souls has three distinguishing characters - as it were a threefold Trademark - Tranquillity, Gentleness, Strength. All our action - and now we are thinking specially of action - must be peaceful, gentle and strong. That suggests, doesn't it? an immense depth, and an invulnerable steadiness as the soul's abiding temper; a depth and a steadiness which come from the fact that our small action is now part of the total action of God, whose Spirit, as another saint has said, "Works always in tranquillity." Fuss and feverishness, anxiety, intensity, intolerance, instability, pessimism and wobble, and every kind of hurry and worry - these, even on the highest levels, are signs of the self-made and self-acting soul; the spiritual parvenu. The saints are never like that. They share the quiet and noble qualities of the great family to which they belong: the family of the Sons of God.

If, then, we desire a simple test of the quality of our spiritual life, a consideration of the tranquillity, gentleness and strength with which we deal with the circumstances of our outward life will serve us better than anything that is based on the loftiness of our religious notions, or fervour of our religious feelings. It is a test that can be applied anywhere and at any time. Tranquillity, gentleness and strength, carrying us through the changes of weather, the ups and downs of the route, the varied surface of the road; the inequalities of family life, emotional and professional disappointments, the sudden intervention of bad fortune or bad health, the rising and falling of our religious temperature. This is the threefold imprint of the Spirit on the souls surrendered to His great action.

We see that plainly in the Saints; in the quiet steadiness of spirit with which they meet the vicissitudes and sufferings of their lives. They know that these small and changing lives, about which we are often so troubled, are part of a great mystery; the life that is related to God and known by God. They know, that is, that they, and all the other souls they love so much, have their abiding place in Eternity; and there the meaning of everything which they do and bear is understood. So all their action comes from this centre; and whether it is small or great, heroic or very homely, does not matter to them much. It is a tranquil expression of obedience and devotedness. As Ornan the Jebusite turned his threshing floor into an altar, they know how to take up and turn to the purposes of the Spirit the whole of life as it comes to them from God's Hand. St. Bernard and St. Francis discard all outward possessions, all the grace and beauty of life, and accept poverty and hardship; and through their renunciation a greater wealth and a more exquisite beauty is given the world. St. Catherine of Genoa leaves her ecstasy to get the hospital accounts exactly right; Elizabeth Fry goes to Newgate, Mary Slessor to the jungle, and Elizabeth Leseur accepts a restricted home life; all in the same royal service.

And we see that all these contrasted forms of action are accepted and performed quietly, humbly and steadily; without reflections about the superior quality of other people's opportunities, or the superior attraction of other people's jobs. It is here that we recognise their real character; as various expressions in action of one life, based on one conviction and desire. Thus there is no tendency to snatch another person's work, or dodge dull bits of their own; no cheapening sense of hurry, or nervous anxiety about success. The action of those whose lives are given to the Spirit has in it something of the leisure of Eternity; and because of this, they achieve far more than those whose lives are enslaved by the rush and hurry, the unceasing tick-tick of the world. In the spiritual life it is very important to get our timing right. Otherwise we tend to forget that God, Who is greater than our heart, is greater than our job too. It is only when we have learnt all that this means that we possess the key to the Kingdom of Heaven.

We have considered that co-operation with the Spirit's action which is to balance our communion with God, as a giving of ourselves to His service, doing some of His work in the world. But there is another and a deeper side: the hidden action of each soul called by God, the effort and struggle of the interior life what we have to do in response to the Love which is drawing us out of darkness into His great light. Even that mysterious communion with God in which we seek, and offer ourselves to, that which we love - in spite of the deep peace it brings - is not without the pain and tension which must be felt by imperfect human creatures, when they contemplate and stretch towards a beauty and perfection which they cannot reach. Still more when it comes to the deeper action, the more entire self-giving, the secret transformation to which that vision of perfection calls us; and the sacrifice, struggle and effort which, sooner or later, this transformation must involve. The Perfection at which the awakened soul gazes is a magnet, drawing him towards itself. It means effort, faithfulness, courage, and sometimes grim encounters if he is to respond to that attraction, and move towards it along the narrow track which leads up and out from the dark valleys of the mind.

I think as I write this of Dürer's wonderful drawing of the Knight, Death and the Devil: the Knight of the Spirit on his strong and well kept horse - human nature, treated as it ought to be, and used as it ought to be - riding up a dark rocky defile. Beside him travels Death, a horrible, doddering figure of decay, saying, "All things perish - time is passing - we are all getting older - is this effort really worth while?" On his flank is a yet more hideous fellow-pilgrim; the ugly, perverse, violent element of our mixed human nature, all our animal part, our evil impulses, nagging at him too. In one way or another, we all hear those two voices from time to time; with their discouragements and sneers, their unworthy invitations, their cynical comments and vile suggestions. "Don't forget me, I am your future," says Death. "Don't forget me," says animal man, "I am your undying past." But the Knight of the Spirit does not look at them. He has had his hand-to-hand struggle farther back; and on his lance is impaled the horrid creature, his own special devil, which he has slain. Now he is absorbed in the contemplation of something beyond the picture, something far more real than the nightmarish landscape through which he must travel; and because of that, he rides steadily forth from that lower world and its phantasies to the Eternal World and its realities. He looks at that which he loves, not at that which he hates, and so he goes safely out of the defile into the open; where he will join the great army of God. There spiritual life as humanity is it; based on the deep conviction that the Good, the Holy, is the Real, and the thing that matters, fed and supported by the steadfast contemplation of the Holy and the Real - which is also the Beautiful and the Sane - and expressed in deliberate willed movements towards it, a sturdy faithful refusal to look at that which distracts us from it. Always looking the same way, and always moving the same way: in spite of obstacles, discouragements, mockery and fatigue. "Thou hast made us for thyself, and our hearts find no rest save in thee." But we must be willing to undertake the journey, whatever it may cost.

Part IV:

Some Questions and Difficulties

There are certain questions and difficulties which turn up again and again in relation to the spiritual life. Of these, one of the most fundamental concerns the Nature of God, and the way in which men should think of Him; and in particular, whether Christians can properly use the word Reality and other terms of an impersonal and philosophic sort as synonyms for God. I think that they can and should do so. In religion, where familiar words so easily lose their full meaning for us, it is often valuable to use other words, though they cannot indeed express the full truth, emphasise other aspects of our great spiritual inheritance. St. Augustine surely answers this question when he says, "God is the only Reality, and we are only real in so far as we are in His order and He in us." St. Augustine was a great Christian. Nothing could exceed the fervour of his personal communion with God. Yet it is the impersonal revelation of a Power and Beauty "never new, yet never old," which evokes his greatest outbursts of adoring joy. The truth is we must use both personal and impersonal language if our fragmentary knowledge of the richness of God's Being is to be expressed; and a reminder of this fact is often a help to those for whom the personal language of religion has become conventional and unreal.

This leads to the next question of importance, which also involves our view of the Nature of God. When we consider the evil, injustice, and misery existing in the world, how can we claim that the ultimate Reality at the heart of the universe is a Spirit of peace, harmony, and infinite love? What evidence can we bring to Support such a belief? and how can we adore a God whose creation is marred by cruelty, suffering and sin?

This is, of course, the problem of evil; the crucial problem for all realistic religion. It is no use to dodge this issue, and still less use to pretend that the Church has a solution of the problem up her sleeve. I would rather say with Baron von Hügel. that Christian spirituality does not explain evil and suffering, which remain a mystery beyond the reach of the human mind, but does show us how to deal with them. It insists that something has gone wrong, and badly wrong, with the world. That world as we know it does not look like the work of the loving Father whom the Gospels call us to worship; but rather, like the work of selfish and undisciplined children who have been given wonderful material and a measure of freedom, and not used that freedom well. Yet we see in this muddled world a constant struggle for Truth, Goodness, Perfection; and all those who give themselves to that struggle - the struggle for the redemption of the world from greed, cruelty, injustice, selfish desire and their results - find themselves supported and reinforced by a spiritual power which enhances life, strengthens will, and purifies character. And they come to recognise more and more in that power the action of God. These facts are as real as the other facts, which distress and puzzle us; the apparent cruelty, injustice and futility of life. We have to account somehow for the existence of gentleness, purity, self-sacrifice, holiness, love; and how can we account for them, unless they are attributes of Reality?

Christianity shows us in the most august of all examples the violence of the clash between evil and the Holiness of God. It insists that the redemption of the world, defeating the evil that has infected it by the health-giving power of love -

bringing in the Kingdom of God - is a spiritual task, in which we are all required to play a part. Once we realise this, we can accept - even though we cannot understand - the paradox that the world as we know it contains much that is evil; and yet, that its Creator is the one supreme Source and Object of the love that will triumph in the end.

Such a view of our vocation as this brings with it another fundamental question. How are we to know, or find out, what the Will of God is? I do not think that any general answer can be given to this. In clear moral and political issues, we must surely judge and act by the great truths and demands of Christianity; and if we have the courage to do this, then, as we act, more and more we shall perceive the direction of the Will. That choice, cause, or action, which is least tainted by self-interest, which makes for the increase of happiness - health - beauty - peace - cleanses and harmonises life, must always be in accordance with the Will of the Spirit which is drawing life towards perfection. The difficulty comes when there is a conflict of loyalties, or a choice between two apparent gods. At such points many people feel unaware of any guidance, unable to discern or understand the signals of God; not because the signals are not given, but because the mind is too troubled, clouded and hurried to receive them. "He who is in a hurry," said St. Vincent de Paul, "delays the things of God." But when those who are at least attempting to live the life of the Spirit, and have consequently become more or less sensitive to its movements, are confronted by perplexing choices, and seem to themselves to have no clear light, they will often become aware, if they will wait in quietness, of a subtle yet insistent pressure in favour of the path which they should take. The early Friends were accustomed to trust implicitly in indications of this kind, and were usually justified.

Where there is no such pressure, then our conduct should be decided by charity and common sense; qualities which are given to us by God in order that they may be used.

Next, we are obliged to face the question as to how the demand of modern psychology for complete self-expression, as the condition of a full and healthy personal life, can be reconciled with the discipline, choice and sacrifice which are essential to a spiritual life; and with this the allegation made by many psychologists that the special experiences of such a spiritual life may be dismissed as disguised wish-fulfilments. In the first place, the complete expression of everything of which we are capable - the whole psychological zoo living within us, as well as the embryonic beginnings of artist, statesman or saint - means chaos, not character. We must select in order to achieve; can only develop some faculties at the expense of others. This is just as true for the man of action or of science as it is for the man of religion. But where this discipline is consciously accepted for a purpose greater than ourselves, it will result in a far greater strength and harmony, a far more real personality, than the policy of so-called self-expression. As to the attempt to discredit the spiritual life as a form of wish-fulfilment, this has to meet the plain fact that the real life of the Spirit has little to do with emotional enjoyments, even of the loftiest kind. Indeed, it offers few attractions to the natural man; nor does it set out to satisfy his personal desires. The career to which it calls him is one that he would seldom have chosen for himself. It proceeds by way of much discipline and renunciation, often of many sufferings, to a total abandonment to God's purpose which leaves no opening even for the most subtle expressions of self-love.

I come now to the many people who, greatly desiring the life of communion with God, find no opportunity for attention to Him

44

in an existence which often lacks privacy, and is conditioned by ceaseless household duties, exacting professional responsibilities or long hours of work. The great spiritual teachers, who are not nearly so aloof from normal life as those who do not read them suppose, have often dealt with this situation; which is not new, though it seems to press with peculiar weight upon ourselves. They all make the same answer: that what is asked of us is not necessarily a great deal of time devoted to what we regard as spiritual things, but the constant offering of our wills to God, so that the Practical duties which fill most of our days can become Part of His order and be given spiritual worth. So Père Grou, whose writings are among the best and most Practical guides to the spiritual life that we possess, says, "We are always praying, when we are doing our duty and turning it into work for God." He adds that among the things which we should regard as spiritual in this sense are our household or professional work, the social duties of our station, friendly visits, kind actions and small courtesies, and also necessary recreation of body and of mind; so long as we link all these by intention with God and the great movement of His Will.

So those who wonder where they are to begin, might begin here; by trying to give spiritual quality to every detail of their everyday lives, whether those lives are filled with a constant succession of home duties, or form part of the great systems of organised industry or public service, or are devoted to intellectual or artistic ends. The same lesson is taught by George Herbert's poem: -

> *Who sweeps a room as for Thy laws,*
> *Makes that and the action fine ...*

and, in a way that brings it home very vividly to modern

minds, by a beautiful letter of Baron von Hügel, which is printed on page fifty-eight of his "Letters to a Niece." This describes how even such a practical activity as packing can be given eternal worth. I do not suggest that this readjustment, this new attitude, can be achieved merely by wishing for it. Nothing which is worth having is as easy as that. It means discipline of thought and of feeling, a more careful use of such leisure as we have; and filling our minds with ideas that point the right way, instead of suggestions which distract us from God and spiritual things. It must also mean some time, even though this may be a very short time, given, and given definitely, to communion with Him; and perseverance in this practice, even though at first we seem to get nothing from it. There are few lives in which there is no pause through the day. We must use even the few minutes that we have in this way, and let the spirit of these few minutes spread through the busy hours. This will also involve expelling from our life those thoughts and acts which are inconsistent with these times of communion. For unless we are prepared to make this the centre of our life, setting the standard to which all the rest must conform, we need not hope for results. We cannot begin the day by a real act of communion with the Author of peace and Lover of concord, and then go on to read a bloodthirsty newspaper at breakfast.

It is this constant correlation between inward and outward that really matters; and this has always been the difficulty for human beings, because there are two natures in us, pulling different ways, and their reconciliation is a long and arduous task. Many people seem to think that the spiritual life necessarily requires a definite and exacting plan of study. It does not. But it does require a definite plan of life; and courage in sticking to the plan, not merely for days or weeks, but for years. New mental and emotional habits must be formed, all our interests re-arranged in new proportion round a new centre. This is something which cannot be hurried; but, unless we take it seriously, can be infinitely delayed. Many people suggest by their behaviour that God is of far less importance than their bath, morning paper, or early cup of tea. The life of co-operation with Him must begin with a full and practical acceptance of the truth that God alone matters; and that He, the Perfect, always desires perfection. Then it will inevitably press us to begin working for perfection; first in our own characters and actions, next in our homes, surroundings, profession and country. We must be prepared for the fact that even on small and personal levels this will cost a good deal; frequently thwarting our own inclinations and demanding real sacrifice.

Here the further question of the relation of spiritual life to public life and politics comes in. It must mean, for all who take it seriously, judging public issues from the angle of eternity, never from that of national self-interest or expediency; backing our conviction, as against party or prejudice, rejecting compromise, and voting only for those who adopt this disinterested point of view. Did we act thus, slowly but surely a body of opinion - a spiritual party, if you like - might be formed; and in the long run make its influence felt in the State. But such a programme demands much faith, hope and charity; and courage too.

finis

THE
SPIRAL WAY

BEING MEDITATIONS UPON
THE FIFTEEN MYSTERIES
OF THE SOUL'S ASCENT

Gyrans gyrando vadit spiritus

*In the Light which fills that secret place is laid up
for us the pattern of our imperishable Crown. It is
made of roses, wild and fragrant, and 'in each rose
is written the word Love.' To that centre we may
retreat . . .*

John Cordelier
(Evelyn Underhill)

Introduction

That jewel in the making, the ever growing crystal of Divine Humanity, seems destined to reflect from every facet some new aspect of the infinitely various Being of God; the inexhaustible simplicity of Christ. Each soul that is added to it, cut and polished by the sharp and steady action of grace, offers a fresh angle to the incoming Divine Light; gives a fresh picture of its love to the world. Yet there is a unity in this variousness; for all are centred on one point, each grows by the laws which rule the universal growth, each draws its very life from one sacred heart. They are one, because they belong to the mystical and eternal fellowship of Jesus. For each to live is Christ; and to grow is to assimilate the simple yet difficult secret of His growth. They are many, since to each His life in them is a separate and peculiar gift, taking character from the temperament through which it is received. Thus His mystical body of many members is built up in our midst.

To its share in the building of that body - to its part in that drama of growth - it is certain that the soul of man is dedicated in advance. Here is the spiritual vocation of the race: a vocation resisted only at the cost of a complete stagnation, of a rejecting of all that is enduring and significant, all that is beautiful and good. That tendency to Deity of which philosophers speak to us, is inherent in our living world of change. There is a Voice that cries to us out of the storm of Becoming: that demands our co-operation, inviting us to great surrender and great joy. The Spirit of Christ sweeps through the world on its journey to the Father: and in virtue of its supreme attraction, its compelling power, catches to itself every lesser spirit on its path. It cries, "Follow! Follow!" to recalcitrant life, lagging behind it: life, ever tending to turn on its own tracks, to be satisfied with something a little lower than its best possible, sinking back upon an inglorious and comfortable past. It entices, and it pursues. "He who loves, knows that Voice," said Thomas à Kempis; and he who hears it, is caught by that cosmic music into the deep enchantment of the lover, for in its cadence is the very sorcery of love. In its accents is celestial beauty; the magical appeal of ecstasy and pain, offering us the final choice between that generous surrender which is heaven and that terrified refusal which is hell. It speaks to us in every growing, changing thing; it speaks in the stars and in the shrouded fields; calling us to a conscious sharing in the mighty business of the spiritual world. It demands incarnation, and seeks for self-expression; not upon some far-off intangible plane of being, but in the here-and-now experience of the race. And the virgin soul hidden somewhere within us recognises it; stirring in her slumbers, as though that insistent Ave of the Universe had reached her through the barriers of the flesh.

According to the deep saying of the theologians, the Father, primal and unconditioned Essence of the God-head, can only know Himself as mirrored in the Son. The undeclared riches of Deity take form in the wisdom of His energetic Word; and God finds Himself in the Eternal Christ. So too the Son, our Friend and Lover, source and pattern of our perfection, broods eternally above humanity, and seeks to see himself mirrored in man's soul. And as from the ecstatic encounter of the two primal aspects of Reality there flashed into being a third form, the Holy Spirit of their Love, whereby the Trinity in Unity was made complete: so another Love, that mystic passion which interweaves Divine and Human nature, is born of the encounter between the Eternal Christ and the spirit of man. This love it is which stings to life a latent thing within us, and sets in hand the supernatural drama of the soul's career.

Because of this all-powerful love, because of that community of interests which it operates, we are a part now of the pageant of Christ's glory: motes, transfigured by the effulgence of His mystical body, our separated lives surrendered to the unresting movement of His will. There comes a moment when a strange new growth begins in us: when we find that we are set on a new path, begin to ascend towards fresh levels of being, now supremely "natural" because inevitable for us, yet closed to our vision in the past. We see before us the footsteps of our companion, showing us where we must tread: passing by many terrible places where our little, human life could never go alone. He moves thus towards His goal, and we must follow; for irresistible love has made us one with Him. He grows thus to His full stature, for He is Very Life: and we, desiring His gift of life in its abundance, must learn its secret if we can. Here, if ever, we see that Life in its wholeness, incarnate, free, and regnant; untainted by disharmonies, growing to its perfect consummation in God. Here the mystery of transcendence is disclosed to us: spirit flaming up and out, through the world of matter, to its goal. In Jesus, that spirit finds its perfect thoroughfare. But in us there is roadmaking to be done, the hard cutting of new paths: only to be accomplished in so far as we follow His methods and grow with His growth.

How, then, shall we grow? and what shall be the curve that marks our progress - that "way," as the mystics call it, which is a journey and a transmutation in one? Where, on the wide horizons or in the inaccessible heavens, lies the goal towards which we are to hew a path? Did we ask this of eager, striving Nature, she would be hard-pressed perhaps to answer us; for her achievements seem to lie in all directions, stretching sheaf-like towards every point. Since God is not Height alone but

Depth and Breadth, transcending yet transfusing all, Life in her flight to Him may take all pathways. Her outgoing, expansive tendency may everywhere achieve success, for He is the Point in which all lines must end. This we see, and all the wonder and the greatness of it: we stand awed and bewildered before her innumerable adjustments and contrivances, her exquisite and complicated arts.

Yet these achievements and these arts are not for us. High above life, yet utterly within it - transcending all its ever-changing beauty, yet that very beauty's energising soul - we discern the Eternal Christ; with whom and in whom we, since we are carried on Life's crest, must surely seek to live. He reigns in virtue of a transcendent vitality, a summing up and excelling of Creation: and we can only achieve union with Him in so far as we are able to grow towards that most human and impassioned self-expression of the victorious life of God. But the transition is too difficult for us. We need a guide and a pathfinder, some merely human thing that went before us through the jungle, and made in our name the essential contact with Reality. We need in fact the natural simplicity of Mary to lead us to our supernatural self-mergence in Christ; maternal life to show us the secret whereby she brought forth in our very midst the Son of God.

Mary, then, protagonist of this great drama, may stand for us as the representative of the race in its mighty encounter with God, the incarnate genius of humanity: its perfect product, and its long-sought dream. She is Life indeed - our life - the very Mother of men. Nourished upon that breast held in safe contact with that homeliness, we may endure without fear our difficult re-birth into a strange universe. Under that mantle of mercy we may struggle up the spiral way on which she passed to her enthronement at the very centre of Reality. "Blessed art

thou among women, and blessed is the fruit of thy womb":
for indeed the holy thing which is born of that surrendered
spirit can be no other than Divine Humanity itself. Here we
see as in a mirror the soul's august possibilities expressed.

So contemplating the image of Mary, so following as it were
with dreamy love the unrolling of the pageant of her soul, bit
by bit the necessary adventures of our own soul on its long
quest of transcendence, become clear. We begin to discern the
intimate construction of our life: the organic laws which must
govern the unfolding of its flower. We begin to see that as the
great drama of Reality is the music of God, so the growing
spirit of man is somewhat like a symphony; that it too has as
its central fact a theme divinely developed, first stated in its
simplicity, then manifested through a movement which is all
strife and passion, bringing ever to richer and deeper expression
by means of that toil and conflict the holy growing theme;
finally, that it has a *reprise* in which the Divine theme transcends
those stormy oppositions, and is lifted to higher levels of
power, of beauty, and of peace. Thesis, Antithesis, Synthesis;
so runs the dialectic of the spirit. As with the mysteries of the
Christian drama, so too with the experience of the individual
soul. In joy, in sorrow, and in triumph the romantic melody of
our inner life is expressed: the "ecclesiastical music" of our
eager yet imperfect imitation of Christ.

Year by year the Christian Church, with life's peculiar
instinct for the recapitulation of her own methods, plays out
this symphony before us; his heavenly story of our growth
in God. From Advent to Assumptiontide it runs: "from
glory to glory advancing" through the joyful mysteries of
Christmas and Epiphany, and the sorrowful mysteries of the
Passion, to the triumphant mystery of Resurrection, and of
that transcendent and eternal life of the deified Spirit which

is heralded by the Easter-fact. A threefold ascent, a spiral way, is then made clear before us, as the pathway from appearance to reality: once fully accomplished in history by our Master, and therefore demanded according to its measure from each awakened soul. The inspiring spirit of this ascent is to be no negative, aloof ejection of that given and apparent world. Rather from first to last, it is a steady uplifting of all things into the order of Divine Reality. The whole of man's nature - will, intellect, and love - is concerned in it: it keeps in warmest human fashion close hold upon the Here and Now. At once a journey, yet a development; a stripping off, yet a completing; a victory, yet a self-loss; only in a paradox can its supernal nature be made clear.

A wholeness, at once Divine and human - the veritable expression of the Eternal in time - is the character of the new life to be aimed at; and at last perhaps to be achieved. It is only by the humble and difficult mystery of growth that attainment can be possible for us: that growth which runs through all creation, the universal and dynamic expression of the Mind of Christ. New life He asks from us; yes! not from us alone, but from every level of creation - new life in bird and tree and creeping thing, new life breaking from the Seed which He has implanted in the soul. Here - not in any static creed, nor any dream-like mystic revelation - is the fulfilment of all meanings, the filling up of the measure of all glory, the disclosing of the final aim of our living and unresting universe.

Yet not alone shall we accomplish it by the inherent energies of that germ of Divine life within. As the mystery of growth in the little human child seems somewhat upspringing from within, yet is actually dependent on nourishment given from without on a friendly universe that upholds and feeds it - so it is with that little child of the Infinite, the soul. The will stretching to God, growing up towards Him as it seems by the vital quality of its love, and carrying with it the whole personality - this must be fed from without, nourished by the Divine Life incessantly poured in on us, if it is to develop, to survive.

> *As the small rain upon the tender grass,*
> *And as the showers upon the herb,*

so is the action of grace upon the growing soul. Grace, then, shall balance growth, and support it: grace, and that vital art of prayer, whereby we appropriate it, opening gates to its inflow, transmuting it into the very substance of our life.

We are not left desolate in this our great adventure. As our bodies in the world of nature, so are our souls immersed and upheld in the world of grace. As the growing tree in the earth, so are we rooted in God. As the flower to the sun, our spirits may open to Him, draw from His infinite strength the power that inspires our growth. "As the shower upon the herb," His Reality is mysteriously distilled upon us: the heavenly food which nourishes His whole creation and is at once the very Bread of Angels and the sustenance of littlest living things. When man first knows this, then he begins to know his wonder and his littleness: to discern the actuality of his sonship, the mystery and beauty of that Immanent Love which holds him safe within Its arms. "Hereby know we that we abide in Him and He in us, because He hath given us of His spirit."

The Joyful Mysteries of the Soul's Ascent

First Joyful Mystery: The Annunciation

Seen from this side the veil, the wonder of the Incarnation is the descent of Godhead to us: yet seen from the standpoint of Eternity, it may well be that the truer wonder is the ascent of our humanity to Him. In the eyes of the angels that boundless generosity is but the meet expression of His nature: *donner est chose naturel à Dieu.* It is rather in Mary's receptivity that these would find the miracle: in that unique example of a perfect response.

Life as they see it, that mounting flood of Spirit ever striving, tending, towards God, here touched Reality at last. So many had gone up the mountain to that one desired encounter; only to be thwarted by the cloud that broods upon the summit, and hides from human eyes the Shining Light within. The great prophets, poets, and philosophers of the antique world - all these had gone up, all had marked classic moments in the ascent of the race. Then came a little girl, pure, meek, and receptive: and ran easily to her destiny and the destiny of the Universe because she was "full of grace." She held out her heart to the Invisible, and in this act flung a bridge across the chasm which separates Illusion from Reality.

Mary becomes by this circumstance the type and pattern of each human soul. Consciously or unconsciously, all are candidates for her high office: all are striving towards the Transcendent, stretching towards the contact of the Divine. She alone, because of her lowliness, "failed not of the prick, the which is God." Sealed and made safe by His touch on her, she remained for all time immaculate - the veritable Sophia, the unspotted virgin, yet the fruitful mother of the soul's true life.

"Quem cum amavero, casta sum,
cum tetigero, munda sunt,
cum accepero, virgo sum!" [1]

This is a part of the great paradox of purity, the shining chastity of love, whereby:

"... Of pure Virgins none
Is fairer seen
Save One
Than Mary Magdalene."

"Hail, Mary, full of grace," said the angel. To him that hath, shall be given. Because Mary was full of grace, to her was vouchsafed the crowning grace of the created order: the life of God upspringing within her, the deification of humanity.

O felix mens et beata anima, quæ te Dominum Deum suum meretur devote suscipere, et in tua susceptione spirituali gaudio repleri! O quam magnum suscipit Dominum, quam dilectum inducit hospitem, quam jucundum recipit socium, quam fidelem acceptat amicum, quam speciosum et nobilem amplectitur sponsum: præ omnibus dilectis, et super omnia desiderabilia amandum! [2]

How hard, we say, for the little human animal to rise to such a height! Yet perhaps it was not very difficult: for she did but carry up to a sublime and simple operation humanity's greatest and most natural activity - the act of prayer. She stretched to God: and where a way is open, He cannot but come in. "Thy opening and His entering are but one moment," said Eckhart, for Spirit waits eternally at the door of the flesh: "and to wait until thou openest is harder for Him than for thee." Only the opposition of our separated will hinders the perpetual incarnation of the Spirit of God: hence Mary's willing receptivity, her humble self-surrender, was the direct condition of the inflow of His Life - that "rippling tide of Divine love" which breaks in light and colour on the human shore, but has behind it the whole weight of the ocean of Godhead, pressing relentless to its bourne. "For the Spirit of God," says Boehme, "goeth with the willing into the soul, it desireth the soul; it setteth its magia towards the soul; the soul needs only to open the door."

"Lift up your heads, O ye gates, and be ye lift up, ye everlasting doors; and the King of glory shall come in. Who is the King of glory? It is the Lord strong and mighty, even the Lord mighty in battle."

Thus does the Announcing Angel cry at the closed door of the heart: and quick behind him, bearing him upon its current, comes the inpouring torrent of the Spiritual Life. "The Lord strong and mighty, even the Lord mighty in battle" - the all-conquering Love, as a rushing wind and as a purging flame, inhabiting the human creature, searching body, soul, and spirit to the deeps, turning purity to ardour, and making of the obedient Maiden the Mother of her Saviour and her God.

But Mary did not hear the splendid periods of that message. For her one phrase was enough. "The Lord *is* with thee": all was told in this. "Thou art full of grace; thy door is open. The Lord is with thee: God is thy possession here and now." When the awakened soul knows this indeed, no more needs to be announced to it. All hangs then on its response. And Mary said: "Behold the handmaid of the Lord, be it unto me according to thy word." Will and grace, which "rise and fall together," here rose to their classic expression and had their perfect work. The soul, says St Bernard, is in essence "a capacity for the Infinite." In this her being, her very existence, consists. That capacity is no mere quality, it is *herself*: and on her acceptance of this, the governing fact of her nature, the whole of her cyclic history depends. "Be it unto me according to thy word." I am human, so a home for Thee.

How then shall it happen to us - this act of self-realisation, this pure impulse of surrender, this first beginning of our new career? Where shall the news of our royal vocation reach us: at what point shall a messenger lean out to us from the sheltering world of spirit, to cry *Dominus tecum* in our astonished ears? We cannot know. In the dreams of the old painters, Gabriel did not always flash upon Mary as she knelt in prayer. Sometimes he found her as she sat musing in the twilight; sometimes as she went to draw water at the well. Sometimes he woke her from sleep in the early morning; or slid within her vision as she worked at her embroidery frame. So too with us. Grace laughs at our little barriers: our artificial separation of sacred from profane. Perhaps we shall hear his murmurous *Ave* in a silent hour of contemplation: perhaps it will come to us, clear and startling, from out the ecstasies of love. It may be in the exultant periods of music, or shining in the eyes of the poor, the maimed, and the unworthy, that the angel of our Annunciation will come. It matters not. Whether that illumination come to us from the altar or from the teeming streets, out of a radiant sky, or from the midst of many sorrows - whether it find us at work or at play, at war with the world or at peace "one thing only is necessary," the instant eagerness of our response.

Domine Deus meus, creator meus, et redemptor meus, cum tali affectu, reverentia, laude et honore, cum tali gratitudine, dignitate et amore, cum tali fide, spe et puritate, te affecto hodie suscipere, sicut te suscepit et desideravit sanctissima mater tua, gloriosa virgo Maria, quando Angelo evangelizanti sibi incarnationis mysterium, humiliter ac devote respondit: Ecce ancilla Domini; fiat mihi secundum verbum tuum. [3]

Second Joyful Mystery: The Visitation

"And Mary arose in those days and went into the hill country with haste." Activity followed close upon the heels of revelation; as if the new dower of vitality poured in on her must somehow be expressed. She could not stay passively in those angel-haunted solitudes, where she had been overshadowed by the power and the presence of God. Not in stillness, in rapt meditation, was the Child Emmanuel to be quickened in her womb. The pendulum of spirit, that swings perpetually between fruition and self-donation - the mysterious give-and-take of the living soul - drove her out into life's arena, and up to the hilltops of prayer: the double movement of the awakened heart.

Three times in the long story of man's transcendence, we are shown the soul driven up into the mountain by the growing spirit within: three times a prayerful ascent to life's summits is shown to be an implicit of the Way. In the mystery of the Visitation that soul goes joyfully and hastily. She seeks of her own volition the hill country: the new life within her stings to instant consciousness the spiritual passion for the heights. Here is the first instinct of the soul that is touched by God. "My beloved spake and said unto me: Rise up, my love, my fair one, and come away." There is but one answer to that heavenly invitation. It is the active, exultant prayer of the neophyte; that unlearned prayer of utmost simplicity and beauty which seems like childish footsteps running up and out towards its home. It is so full of gladness, charged with gratitude and trust, that the very labour of ascent becomes a joy: "for He that is mighty hath magnified me, and holy is His name."

In another mood than this the adult and heroic Christian must bear the cross uphill towards his death in God: in another glory, power, and beauty ascend at last from the Mount of

Vision to the ecstatic union with Reality. But the time for these things is not yet: a merciful cloud covers them. The soul at the beginning of her course dreams not of the sorrows and the triumphs that must attend upon her steady growth in prayer.

But there is another aspect of this outgoing of Mary from her home. She goes, not only to God, but to Man. Charity has been engendered in her, and already demands expression under two orders: in Service and in Adoration, the life of active love, the life of prayer. The quickening of that mysterious Divine life within sharpens her ears to the call of the human life without: already she is reminded that she cannot sever her experience from that of the race. Humility, and its flower, which is Courtesy, spring up within her: the first unfolding fronds of the new growth. This is an earnest of the reality of her vocation; the supernal nature of her destiny as bridge-builder between two worlds. So she goes up into the hill country in a spirit of prayer, yet goes upon a simple human errand, love Divine and human interwoven in her outlook from the first: and humanity, simple yet far-seeing, comes to meet her with a blessing on its lips. Filled with an exultant consciousness of new and crescent life she goes: possessed of a joy so lyrical in quality that it can only find expression in a song. "And Mary said: My soul doth magnify the Lord, and my spirit hath rejoiced in God my Saviour." It is the greatest poem of Christendom, yet from homeliest natural intercourse its ecstatic periods are born. The music of the Magnificat springs out of the very heart of life.

In that hour of the Divine Office which looks forward to the coming day as yet unborn, the coming life implicit but unseen, the striving, growing Church - at once type and mother of all Christians - takes upon her lips this exultant, passionate song. She speaks then, as it seems, for every soul that has learned her secret, that participates in her mystical life: for the hungry filled, for the lowly so wondrously exalted, for each humble human creature who has felt the vivifying touch of love Divine. Yet we ask ourselves as we listen to those rapturous declarations, whether mere humanity, however pure, meek, and Godward-tending, were capable of such a song as this? Rather it seems as though the Magnificat were the first earnest of the Incarnation: truth apprehended under the veils of poetry before it could be recognised in the garment of flesh. Here Christ, finest flower of the Divine Immanence, sings and prays by our side; even whilst He grows within our hearts. It was not with such high poetry, so magical a touch upon reality, that Mary could have replied to Gabriel's message. A world of experience lies between the meek surrender of *Ecce ancilla Domini* and the exaltation of *Magnificat anima mea*. Now, she and her God inextricably entwined together in the common life He shall redeem, she knows that it is with her as His word proclaimed: and can afford to exult because all generations shall call her the blessed, the supremely happy, the Pioneer of the race on its steady growth towards its home. "And His mercy is on them that fear Him, throughout all generations": - yea! on all those, my daughters in the spirit, who have shared their Mother's experience: all those who, taught by me, have opened their hearts to the inflowing Spirit of God. All these shall rise up and call me blessed, for I am the Church, their nursing Mother, I am Life, running to meet her Maker and her Love. I am Wisdom, Mother of all fair things. See my descendants, carrying my secret life through the centuries: Gertrude and Julian, Catherine and Teresa, those handmaidens of Perfect Love, whose low estate He has regarded indeed. See them grow with my growth, and share my sorrows and my triumphs. A Rod sprang from Jesse. Out of the virginal heart of Mary springs the very Tree of Life. "Behold, a virgin shall be with child, and shall bring forth a son, and they shall call his name Emmanuel, which being interpreted is God with us."

Of growth, then, this mystery speaks to us: the hidden, secret, yet unhindered growth of the buried seed. The soul has accepted its destiny: now "according to His Word" the irresistible process of its life goes on. In this living, growing world, this place of passionate efflorescence, where the great trees stand like spreading flames, and every humble plant, each furred and finned and feathered thing, has by its gift of growth a part in the great process of God - here of a sudden, Spirit, which is to say Life in its sublimest aspect, has started into being within the web of visible creation. A seed has germinated that shall indeed "grow up, and become greater than all herbs and shoot out great branches": branches that shall reach to highest heaven, and bridge the gap that separates two worlds.

> "'Fiorito è Cristo nella carne pura,
> or se ralegri l'umana natura.
> Natura umana, quanto eri scurata,
> ch' al secco fieno tu eri arsimigliata!
> Ma lo tuo sposo t' ha renovellata,
> or non sie ingrata
> de tale amadore,
> Tal amador è fior de puritade,
> nato nel campo de verginitade,
> egli è lo giglio de l'umanitade,
> de suavitate
> e de perfetto odore." [4]

Third Joyful Mystery: The Nativity

"The days were fulfilled that she should be delivered": not by any sudden miracle, by any cataclysmic break with nature, but according to the steady and unhurried processes of Life. All specialisation of the Divine is here discounted: and the world's supreme revelation, linking itself with the world's diurnal cares and sweetest natural outbirths, "fulfils the days" and comes forth into the World of Appearance gently, naturally; conforming to the law of living things. That revelation comes, it is true, from the Transcendent; it is a spark from off the altar of the Universe, a veritable scintilla of the Life of God. Yet it buries itself in the world of things, willingly immanent in the human, in so far as that human dwells within the circle of its power.

"He is not the God of philosophers and scholars," said Pascal. No: but "the God of Abraham, the God of Isaac, the God of Jacob" - of simple natural life, of flocks and herds, of seeking, dreaming, wrestling, restless man. *Hoc vobis signum*: the young girl, the little baby, the carpenter, the stable, and the patient beasts. The news told rather in sheepfold than in sanctuary; the Glory of the Lord, the mystic Shekinah, withdrawn from the Holy of Holies to shine upon the fields - here are the signs that God indeed is with us, these are the chosen *media* which declare His will to men. *O magnum mysterium et admirabile sacramentum, ut animalia viderent Dominum natum, jacentem in præsepio.* [5]

Spiritual intuition has always preserved clear consciousness of all that waits upon this Birth: the sudden passionate exultation of the angelic world, all its charitable desires at last fulfilled, all the sacramental manifestation of created things, leading, pointing, to the Crib. Heaven and earth embracing one another: the very being of humanity, its manhood, crowned by this incarnation, and snatched up to a correspondence with the Real. Solemnly announced and long prepared, yet when the hour strikes, when that new life, veritably our own, is seen before us, and "Man stands in the New Birth": then all that had gone before is obliterated, all gives place to this, to "the wonder of wonders, the human made Divine."

The long, strange months of our expectation are over: that hidden certain trust of ours, that joyous consciousness of crescent spirit "our own yet not our own," is justified at last. It is justified in the actual outbirth and appearance of that most real and mystic Life; which is so profound just because it is so simple, so far above us just because it is so divinely near.

> *Welcome all wonders in one sight,*
> *Eternity shut in a span,*
> *Summer in winter, day in night,*
> *Heaven in earth, and God in man,*
> *Great little one, whose all-embracing birth*
> *Lifts earth to heaven, stoops heaven to earth."*

Hodie Christus natus est! hodie salvator apparuit. [6] Suddenly our eyes are unsealed, and we perceive the Eternal Christ living in and for and with us; heaven waiting here and now upon our vision of it; the coming of the Kingdom that is within. We know once for all that the angels need not to come, since they are ever present - "Turn but a stone, and start a wing!" This we know, because the Son of God at last is brought to birth in us. Bethlehem is to us the gateway of the Kingdom of Heaven.

In this hour we feel and know the stirring as it were of a new Life; veritably our own, yet not of us, intimate and dear, yet august and incomprehensible. We experience all the effort and struggle of birth, its uncertainties and fears: bringing forth, as it seems from the womb of personality, that "Starry Stranger" whose advent shall give meaning to our life. Is it we who are changed by that which is worked in us? We cannot tell: but another epoch is now begun for us, another creature - childish and weak, yet like-minded to Christ - looks through our eyes upon a transfigured world. That world is now seen by us "apparelled in celestial light," saturated with Divine possibilities; hampered by matter, yet agleam with God. Of this world we know ourselves, reborn, to be the microcosm. That new life of ours, that thing we have brought forth: this, too, is full of infinite possibilities, a thing of potential freedom linked to somewhat that is not free. We know that He is indeed the Son of the Highest and playmate of the angels. Yet His nurture is confided to our care. It is of the essence of this Divine revelation, working in and through the processes of life, that it comes to us not ready-made, not finished and completed, but surrounded by the halo of a helplessness which calls for our self-giving love. All now seems left to our maternal offices. Shelter we must give, and nourishment. God has sprung up for us, out of the earth as it seems, from the very heart of humanity. Life of our lives, He takes our growing life upon Him: all He gives, and all demands. "He hath not abhorred the Virgin's womb" nor disdained to make the very stuff of our manhood a link in the process of His Immemorial Plan. He will climb by our sides up the great ladder of Becoming. He will grow with our growth toward that supernal life which all shall have in Him. So great is the confidence of our God in those that seek Him, that He has placed within our hands the awful power of marring the image of Divinity.

> *Le plus infirme des pécheurs peut découronner,*
> *peut couronner*
> *Une espérance de Dieu."*

As the mother's life is merged in her child, finds in that child its meaning, and through that child's adventure gleans its most searching and exalted experiences of joy and grief: so now the focus of the soul's history shifts from Mary to Jesus - from the natural life entinctured by overshadowing spirit, to the veritable Spirit-Life new born. The growing Christ is now to be the centre of our story; to exhibit the forward thrust of life, to bear its yoke. "Unto us a Child is born, unto us a Son is given, and the government shall be upon His shoulder."

When we know this, when this gift and this vocation are clear to us, we think that we are at the beginning of glory; since "Heaven itself lies here below," and nothing can dim its joy. Yet perhaps it may be that we are rather at the beginning of woes. The strange new thing in our arms, the little Child of the Infinite mysteriously born of us, has secret affinity with that inexorable Life which came to bring, not peace, but a piercing sword. "Glory to God in the highest, and on earth peace to men of goodwill." This, we say, is the heavenly comment on that Birth. Peace? Yes, to men of goodwill, men of selfless and surrendered desire, whose hearts are at one with the Transcendent, and accept all that is ministered to them at the hand of generous life. But the Church, when she took upon her lips that spiritual song, made thereto significant additions, that she might fit it to her daily needs. That which she begins in exaltation she continues in humility, in a declaration of our meek dependence on Immanent Grace. And suddenly she cries out to that perfect symbol of surrender, to that Lamb of God whose self-donation alone can take the taint of imperfection from the world. Now, even at this moment, when we seem to have all that we dare ask and more, our helplessness and need of Him is clear to us - "Thou that takest away the sin of the world, receive our prayer!" "For Thou only art holy, Thou only art the Lord." Already the soul's Friend and Companion has gone before it to the altar - the only path to union with the Father that is possible to the unruly human heart.

Fourth Joyful Mystery: The Presentation in the Temple

"And when the days of her purification according to the law of Moses were accomplished, they brought Him to Jerusalem to present Him to the Lord."

Changeful, unresting life, inexorable in its progress, its onward push, drove them out into the busy world. Humility, the crown of royal love, drove them to a courteous acquiescence in the rites and forms ordained of other men.

Here, then, in this mystery, the secret adventure of the spirit so deeply hidden "with Christ in God" suddenly emerges as it were into the open: takes its place in the great flux of the universal Becoming, commits itself to the seething tides of human life. There comes a moment when the wonderful thing we have borne, the Life we have cherished, can no longer be concealed. Whether we will or no, the push of Divine Love, which operates its growth in us, sends us out with it into the world; and we must go up, as Mary, to the temple that is in Jerusalem, must bring the new life we have borne into contact with the diurnal actuality of things.

How secret till this hour has been the soul's experience: held within the homely circle of consciousness, defended by the banners of love from the enquiring gaze of other men! Now that soul must go out to those other men, meet their curious or indifferent gaze with courage: it is the first intimation of those heroic and self-giving activities to which the new life is dedicated in advance. "Every ascent to God implies a descent in charity to man." We cannot lie for ever sequestered from the tyrannous ceremony, the tiresome, orderly processes of life. We are bound to accomplish the "liturgy of love," offering our sacrifice "according to that which is said in the law of the Lord." The royal instinct of donation must be fostered from the first, even by the hard and difficult exposure of our treasure to the apathetic gaze of the world: the giving up of our little winged and dove-like thoughts, their wild and delicate magic, to the prosaic demands of a formal creed.

It is not a small sacrifice that is here exacted, in this first emergence from the nest where the soul had its secret to itself. So dear to it have been the solemn fields and the rough stable: the hiddenness and silence, the friendly neighbourhood of simple natural things. But the days are accomplished, and a road goes out of Bethlehem towards Jerusalem; towards the great centre of national, social, credal life. That organized and busy life does not seem to want us: it is well satisfied with the fruits of civilisation, has delimited the mutually exclusive spheres of "flesh" and "spirit," built and fenced in its temple, established its discreetly ceremonial cult of a far-away Divinity, decided on its attitude to God. Of us it makes only one demand: that we shall acquiesce in its ritual, become one of the obedient crowd. We must tame our wild joyousness, put our romantic passion into blinkers: conform, in fact, to the ecclesiastical ideal. Thus, we learn in amazement, was the "Light that lightens the Gentiles" first made known to men; by this humble submission of Life to the demands of tradition, this interweaving of liberty with authority, of the present with the past. "Take My yoke upon you and learn of Me, for I am meek and lowly of heart - surrender is My secret first and last"; and here already at the opening of its course the soul begins to learn it, submitting the liberty it has in Christ to the formulæ which seek to mediate Him to men.

True, there is here no real dimming of the inward joy, for our Love goes with us: yet there is a certain declination from that exultant state of rapture, that lyrical delight in which we have borne and nurtured It, as the curve of the spiral road takes us down towards the world. The little Child of the

Infinite seems to us ill at ease amongst the formal splendours of the Temple. "Love's architecture is His own"; but these man-made walls, so oppressively sure of their "consecrated office," stand about Him as a prison, rather than as a home: shut Him from His sunlit palace of the day. In these stately aisles a shyness falls between us: we no longer speak together as we did. Certainly, we think, the road is trending downwards: the heavenly consciousness, though still we hold it tightly, changes, and threatens to grow dim. Yet, what though we lose that intimate and exquisite communion? This is but the accident, not the substance, of our veritable life in God. "All visions, revelations, and heavenly feelings," says St John of the Cross, "and whatever is greater than these, are not worth the least act of humility, bearing the fruits of that charity which neither values nor seeks itself, which thinketh well not of self but of others."

In the spirit of humility then, bearing in its arms the Fruit of that charity which neither values nor seeks itself, the soul is to go to the world which awaits it: "thinking well" of its laws and its customs, gladly conforming to its least demands. And here, for once, the world repays its generosity. Coming to it with its Treasure, it is met with the acclamation of the seekers and the seers. "He hath exalted the humble and meek": once again, as at the Visitation, simple courtesy is given its reward. The eyes of the race are quick to discern our secret: in the vivid, piercing vision of its dreamers, the eager glance of those who wait and hunger for a glory that shall be revealed. They recognise the strangeness we bear with us, conceal it though we may. "My Secret to myself": it is the very watchword of the mystic. But Simeon, that steadfast, patient watcher on the threshold of revelation, breaks through the soul's defences and divines the wonder of the Thing upon its breast; and cries to his God and ours in an ecstacy of selfless gratitude, "Mine eyes have seen Thy salvation!"

Thus from first to last our solidarity with the race is to be impressed on us. With each new phase of growth, with the declaration of each fresh mystery, the call of humanity rings afresh in our ears. Elizabeth in the hill-top town; the glad shepherds running to the stable; wild nature and sweet homeliness demanding of the soul their share in its wonder and its joy. Self-mergence in the traditions of the multitude, free and generous self-revelation - however much we hate it - to the eyes of those who truly seek: here is to be our duty and our delight. By self-giving we grow, by glad spending we grow rich in Him, by burning, our Light grows brighter - "a Light to lighten the Gentiles, and the Glory of Thy people Israel."

Fifth Joyful Mystery: The Child Amongst the Doctors

The three offices of the angels, said Dionysius the Areopagite - the three properties of that spiritual energy, that prevenient grace which hems us in - were to purify, to illuminate, to perfect, those souls which they cherished and controlled. To each of these great businesses one stage of the Mystic Way was given; Purgative, Illuminative, Unitive. These mark the soul's growth, its steady transmutation, under the pressure of grace, the action of angelic love. The joyful mysteries of spiritual childhood are the mysteries of purification; of the emergence of the real, its subordination of the unreal and the imperfect in us - the birth and establishment of the pure spirit of our Master, the Lordship of Love. Now, that stage draws to an end. We begin to look forward to the path of Illumination; the way, we think, of knowledge and clear sight.

We are growing, stretching out in all directions. Will, intellect, and love are waxing strong; and suddenly we see, as a dazzling vision, wisdom and understanding awaiting us, enticing with their promise, ready as we think to snatch us from the dim, uncertain world of intuition, and satisfy our new and arrogant demand that we may *know*. We hear the voice of Wisdom in the streets, crying -

> *"Come! eat ye of my bread,*
> *And drink ye of the cup that I have mingled,"*

and know that she invites us to a heavenly table; though we little guess the place where that Banquet shall be set, or the bitterness of that Cup of Blessing in which she shall communicate to us of the Life of God. So we loose the hand of Life our Mother, and run to find knowledge amongst the doctors - knowledge of God and man: having yet to learn that the only Way of Illumination for immortal yet imprisoned spirit is the way of pain and growth and love.

It is a childish ignorance: yet even in the progress of our Master and Forerunner we see one incident which confirms this instinct of the growing soul, to seek in mere knowledge some clue to the mystery of life. In His proving of all things He went before us, even on this false scent of the questing spirit; *non necessitate, sed caritate trahente.* [7] Being made man even as we are, He did not disdain man's method of discovery through mistake. But this adventure does not belong to the immense activities of His Manhood: it is rather the one type-act of spiritual immaturity, set for us as a symbol of "the years of childish things." It is a part, too, of the education of the Heavenly Child within us, a schooling in humility, a healthful throw-back to the fundamental realities; a hint to us that our best-intentioned wilful choices are of little account in the great purposes of God. "When I was a child, I spake as a child, I understood as a child, I thought as a child." The child Christ fancied that He was about His Father's business, when He disputed with the theologians in the temple porch; and tried, by the exploration of their traditional wisdom, to discover the secret of that mysterious Life which He felt already, but did not understand. He left the actualities of human experience for the abstractions and the subtleties of the intellectual world. At once He was "lost" in respect of humanity: the virgin soul that had borne the Divine Seed and cherished it, now sought for its traces in vain.

Thus the crescent spirit of the new man early begins to seek the path on which it must travel: coming to the end of the first stage of its journey, it looks eagerly for the next turn on the way. In something *known*, some secret wisdom imparted - a revelation given perhaps to the insistent neophyte, but guarded from the crowd by those who keep its shrine, an inward mysterious meaning evoked from a moribund tradition - here, many imagine that they see their first chance of transcendence: forgetting that the one essential secret is revealed not to intelligent scholars, but to growing babes. They dream of an initiation, some magical "Open Sesame" of the spiritual world; a ready-made solution that shall relieve them from the dreadful obligation of growing into truth. This solution, they think, once they have found it, will lift the cloud from off the mountain, rend the sanctuary veil. They know not that this veil shall only be parted when the soul dies upon the cross, "resisting interior temptation even to despair." So they run eagerly along the way of knowledge: only to find a blind alley, where they looked in their childish optimism for the mighty thoroughfare that leads to God. Then Maternal

Life must seek them sorrowing. Having found them, she takes them by the hand and leads them home; there to grow strong in the spirit, subject to Nature's firm yet gentle ruling, "Safe amongst shadowy, unreal human things."

One and all, we go up to the Temple of Knowledge in the natural enthusiasm and trust of youth. We see it in all its splendour. We hear of the Holy of Holies about which it is built. There, we think, is clearly our destination. There, could we but demand it by the one sufficing question, is the secret which we desire. We believe in the saving power of intellect; and fancy that the encounter of Edipus with the Mistress of the Woven Song is but another version of the soul's supreme encounter with its God. Poor, bewildered, clever children, we sit amongst the doctors; believing ourselves ever to be upon the eve of a revelation which does not come. "All who hear us are astonished" - hear our eager, wistful questions, charged with passion, coming out of the very heart of life to shatter themselves against the impregnable fortifications of the academic mind. Yet the Reality which we seek has but one message for us. "I am the Food of the fullgrown: *grow*, that you may feed on Me." Wisdom's table veritably awaits us, but the way thereto is by another road than this. Clinging to the skirts of life, we must follow where she leads us: through

> *"Shadowy-peopled Infancy,*
> *Through Death and Birth to a diviner day."*

Not by dint of any second-hand knowledge administered to us, any learned "raunsaking of the Divine Majestie," but by humble submission to the slow and steady processes of growth, shall we at last attain

> *"Realms where the air we breathe is love,*
> *Which in the winds on the waves doth move,*
> *Harmonising this earth with what we feel above."*

To an ascent towards Jerusalem, which the mystics called the City of Contemplation, our new birth, our secret life, we think, was aimed. There, it is true, is our final destination: yet the goal of our journey is not the hill of Zion, with its temple and its ceremonial altar, but another place of sacrifice, the hill of Calvary, the harsh and lonely altar of the Cross. To this we shall come when the hour strikes for us: seeking, not knowledge, but place of utmost self-surrender, in majesty and lowliness making the soul's imperial progress to the grave. When we come at last to that mysterious region, the clever intellect must stay without. But love and desire will enter in: the soul's impassioned desire to give all for God. "If thou wouldst know then what this desire is," says Hilton, "verily it is Jesus, for He worketh this desire in thee, and giveth it thee; and He it is that desireth in thee, and He it is that is desired; He is all, and He doth all, if thou couldst see Him. Behold Him well, for He goeth before thee, not in bodily shape, but insensibly, by secret presence of His power. Therefore see Him spiritually if thou canst, and fasten all thy thoughts and affections to Him, and follow Him wheresoever He goeth; for He will lead thee the right way to Jerusalem, that is, to the sight of peace and contemplation."

We are but at the beginning of this our true and only pilgrimage: but our Master and our Love is with us, to show us the "right way." To "follow Him wheresoever He goeth" is the only knowledge that we need. He leads us now to Nazareth; to simple, homely life. Not the head but the heart is the spirit's growing-point. Divine Humanity will not attain to manhood's stature, power, and courage by anything taught, told, or shown; but by difficult choices made and work honestly done. The carpenter's bench is a better instrument of transcendence than the seat amongst the doctors in the temple porch: that

"Strong Son of God, Immortal Love," whom we must follow, was not a product of the schools. He went home and *grew*: humbly learning to do hard and solid work. "All kinds of skill," says Tauler, "are gifts of the Holy Ghost" : and they may bring forth the fruits of that Spirit in those who seek to acquire them in full submission of will and gladness of heart. Christ comes with us to the workshop. With our hands we may learn of Him the fashioning of the Cross: and in learning may learn too those great lessons of patience and endurance, of industrious and courageous love, which will strengthen our muscles to bear its burden in the end.

On this note of acquiescence, of surrender to the steady process of diurnal life, the acceptance of a deeply human education, the joyful mysteries of the soul come to an end. As rain and frost and wind can make the mountain a more lovely thing than any earthly artist's pictured dream; so it is from the friction of daily life that the summits of the soul shall emerge in their triumphant loveliness. Not some esoteric and deliberate art of sculpture, taught to the adepts of an ancient wisdom but hidden from the great desirous crowd; rather, the steady action of the simplest natural forces - summer and winter, storm and sunlight, dew and drought - shall carve their gross contours according to the mind of the Artist, fret out their lofty pinnacles with its faery magic; and give them, when the times are accomplished, the unearthly beauty of the spiritual heights.

The Sorrowful Mysteries of the Soul's Ascent

First Sorrowful Mystery: The Agony In The Garden

The ending of the joyful mysteries is the ending of the childhood of the soul. From the sweet and honest industries of Nazareth, it is flung into the furnace of manhood. The angel that once announced to us new life, now cries in our ears a sterner message: *Viriliter agite* - be a man - if indeed you would be the hidden child of God. With short interval for placid service, for any of those agreeable activities which our comfortable self-indulgence calls "life," the secret passionate and dolorous mysteries of Divine humanity begin.

In our childhood we asked for knowledge, little knowing what we sought. Now knowledge is indeed to come to us; knowledge by union, direct and poignant, by participation in the passion of our Incarnate God. The soul who has experienced the joys of the first dawning, the birth and the nurture, of her hidden life, finds that the next stage of her progress shall be an actual sharing in the redemptive pains of Christ. How, indeed, should it be otherwise? What other solution could our love endure? *Si nihil contrarium vis pati, quomodo eris amicus Christi?* [8] It is a forced option; to suffer either the loss of His friendship or the burden of His griefs. We cannot hesitate in this decision. No second choice competes with this great honour of following in His footsteps if we can. All else - all success or joy or service - is but a shadow-show: a children's game.

"When I became a man," says Paul, "I put away childish things." The intellectual subtleties, the "religious ideas" pondered and played with at the feet of Gamaliel, crumbled to dust at the sight of Stephen's joy and agony. Then "God was pleased to reveal His Son in me," the light "shone out of darkness," the latent spark flamed up. Then Paul, made ardent by the fire of love, suddenly initiated into the mystery of life, went out into that world to which he was crucified; from glory to glory advancing, yet so as by suffering shame and death. "Troubled on every side," he went, "yet not distressed; perplexed, but not in despair; persecuted, but not forsaken; cast down, but not destroyed; always bearing about in the body the dying of the Lord Jesus, that the life also of Jesus might be made manifest in our body."

As the Church in her year-long drama turns from the Crib to begin at once her journey to the Cross, and puts on the royal purple of penance as Epiphany draws to a close: so it is in the intimate drama of that growing and ascending soul in whom "the life of Jesus shall be made manifest." The slow growing up of the Divine within it, the radiant pressure of an Immanent Love transforming the workshop and the home, comes to its term. "Thou hast been too long a child at the breast, a spoiled child," said the Eternal Wisdom to Suso. Spoiled indeed, and lapped too deep in comfort, if we cannot hear in the inexorable voice that calls us from the nursery, the very accents of industrious and courageous love.

It is out in the open, away from all protection, in a moment of effort, of deliberate choice, that the mysterious transfusion of man's spirit by the more living spirit of Christ - His transcendent Manhood entincturing it - is first to be felt and recognised. "Our wills are ours to make them Thine": this is the meaning of man's liberty, the secret spring of the process which takes him back to God. "Be it unto me according to Thy word," said the soul at her amazing initiation into the new life; "Not my will, but Thine, be done," says the Godward-tending spirit that was born of her, at the moment in which a new stage of life's ascent must be attacked. The sanctified will, the attention orientated to the great interests of Reality, never to the fears and anguish of the Self; this primal necessity of all transcendence is brought home to us at each crisis in the history of the soul.

These crises, these sudden and terrible declarations of our freedom, and of the price that freedom exacts - the making of a voluntary choice - always come upon the spirit in an hour in which it is turned towards Reality: in an hour, that is to say, of actual, if not of conscious prayer. Mary's surrender to Life's inflow; the temptation of Jesus, His crucial choice between power and humble love; now the agony in this garden of olives. Here the soul has come, perhaps, to seek its opportunity of utmost joy and of profound communion in the whispering darkness, that dim "place where lovers lose themselves"; withdrawing a space from all others, the better to talk with Him alone. It looks for its Love, awaits the glimmering light, the touch, the heavenly silence: and suddenly it is face to face with the unseen Event towards which it has been growing - the Choice, the dreadful prerogative of the free. Not the primary choice of the temptation in the wilderness, between ambition and service, between power and love; but the final choice, as it seems, between life and death, success and failure, when the Cup of Tribulation is offered by the gentle yet unfaltering Hand of God.

That first great choice of adult spirit was made in the solitudes, amongst wide spaces and austere. Then, by a merciful dispensation, all the complexities of life and growth were cleared away; and the three mighty possibilities of all-powerful yet ill-directed will, were set against the arid background of things. It was the choice between the Divine slavery of the consecrated heart and the human liberty of self-sufficient mind: between the Suffering Servant of the old prophet and the Superman of the new.

But the second, deeper choice that comes on us now - the choice between life and death, success and failure - comes out of the very heart of growing, fertile life. Not as servants but as sons we make it: for the days of our bondage are over, and Christ has made us free. It comes at the end of those joyful mysteries which have assured us of our powers. Much was then given us: now much shall be asked of us again. It shall be made in the midst of a garden, among delicate and lovely living things; radiant now to our exalted consciousness with a transcendent beauty "of splendour in the grass, of glory in the flower" and shining on us through the night which veils our anguish from the world. It shall be made lying prostrate on the kindly turf, pushing to our clenched hands the little hidden flowers, those royal things that need not toil or spin, cease not in their quiet maternal tasks. All about us stand the trees, our silent comrades; vibrant with the upward-pulsing sap, budding in every twig with a life that shall carry on the mystery of creation when we have gone down into the terrible and destined grave. At such an hour the flaming course of spirit seems poor beside the steady march of life.

Yet because here *is* natural life, undeflected by our petty wilfulness, by the twisting, crooked action of our thought, these things among which we suffer seem to help us. The self-giving that we strive for is natural too; it is the very crown of life, the goal of created things. All life, then, is with us as we try to turn to God: for the earnest expectation of the creature waits for the manifestation of His sons. These our companions have their being in Him: their delicate magic falls as clearly within the circle of His will as the difficult growth to which our tortured spirits must conform. So the murmurous voices of the night speak to us of a certain consolation; and our Mother Earth is with us, as she was with our Forerunner, in our prayer. "How beautiful are Thy tabernacles, O Lord of Hosts!" How beautiful the starry tent enverdured with wild olive, where we meet Thy angel in the night!

> ' "Into the woods my Master went,
> Clean forspent, forspent;
> Into the woods my Master came,
> Forspent with love and shame.
> But the olives they were not blind to Him;
> The little grey leaves were kind to Him.
> The thorn tree had a mind to Him
> When into the woods He came.
> Out of the woods my Master went,
> And He was well content;
> Out of the woods my Master came,
> Content with death and shame.
> When death and shame would woo Him last
> From under the trees they drew Him last:
> 'Twas on a Tree they slew Him last
> When out of the woods He came."

What, then, is the true nature of this trial that initiates us into the sublime mysteries of sorrow? It is not hardship that we fear, the laborious life of service; for love is always industrious, though it be not always brave. But frustration, failure, death - *this* is the Cup offered to us: the horrible verdict of futility, uttered as it seems in the deeps of our spirits, the mocking response of an inimical universe to our tentative declarations of new life. To lead other men to the high pastures of holiness and peace, to continue in that ministry of healing confided to the illuminated soul: or else, to go down alone to the encounter of utmost humiliation, surrendering, as it seems, all hope of helping those who depended on us, that so as by fire we may save them in the end - this is the alternative of Gethsemane, and so bitter it is that even our divine Companion can only cry, "Father, let *this* Cup pass!"

It is an alternative that none are strong enough to encounter, unless defended by the heavenly armour of utmost acquiescence in the will of God. The Christ within here cries to Christ without for succour. The soul turns in horror from this destiny of frustration; seeing before it so many possibilities of happy service, feeling and knowing its power to help and heal. But human efficiency, well loved of the short-sighted creature, is not here the Creator's promise to His sons. There is indeed no "promise," no "covenant"; only a demand upon our trust and courage. A self-donation that seems useless is asked of us: a self-donation not inspired by any foresight of the bliss that tribulation may win for us, any commercial scheme of salvation bought at a price, but by an utterly surrendered love, a naughting of the separated will. "Nevertheless, not my will, but Thine, be done"; annihilation itself, so it please Thee.

Yet there is for the Christian soul an ecstasy even in this torment. *Quando ad hoc veneris, quod tribulatio tibi dulcis est, et sapit pro Christo; tunc bene tecum esse æstima, quia invenisti paradisum in terra.* [9] All the Spirits of God are about it; leaning out from that Paradise of theirs, dark to it now, yet in which that soul also has its place. The joyful song of the exultant angels rejoicing in the upward march of life, supports it in its agony: penetrating grief and calming fear. And here once more in the darkness of the garden, just because of this renewed receptiveness, this acceptance of the chalice of pain, grace is veritably poured in on it, as in the first feeble hours of its new life. No more "as small rain upon the tender grass" it comes, but as the hard and drenching showers which hurt to heal - an extra dower of vitality, given at the beginning of sorrows; lest, deprived of that heavenly viaticum, man should faint and fall by the way.

> ' *"Soul of the acorn buried in the sod,*
> *Lord of high trees and sunset-haunted hills,*
> *Planter of primroses and very God*
> *Of the bright daffodils,*
> *Pity the weakness of the growing grain,*
> *And drench our fields with rain!"*

Second Sorrowful Mystery: The Scourging

Fiat voluntas tua. The soul has made its choice: the terrible choice between its personal well-being and subservience to the inscrutable necessities of God. "Not my will, but Thine": my will shall be transmuted into love, "as iron thrust in the fire takes on the semblance of the flame," that so it may be utterly remade in Thee. Wonderful though my separate life has seemed, enlightened by God, and full of opportunities for service, I give it back to Thee now; merge it in the movement of the All. This was the choice made in Gethsemane. Now, that choice is to be carried into action, to find expression in the concrete world of things.

If we have indeed dared to accept the Chalice of Life - of intensest life - which was there offered to us, we have accepted it with all its implications. How then is this choice to be actualised, how exhibited in the growing soul's experience? How can we show our will's surrender; and what gift shall we bring to prove the quality of our love?

Our surrender shall be exhibited by a total self-abandonment, a willing meek acceptance of the lowest place in that School of Perfect Resignation of which the mystics tell us: an acceptance of the commonplace and ignominious suffering which is so easily meted out to us by an inimical or an indifferent world. Our gift of love shall be our whole selves offered up to Him: body, soul, and spirit on the altar, where He has been before. We must go out from the quiet garden of prayer: from that place of dim fragrance where the lover can speak directly to the heart of Beloved. As the exultant hour of the Annunciation is followed on the spiral by a return to the homely courtesies of life, so the sacred moment of heroic choice in which the sorrowful way opens before us, is followed closely by the hardest of all mortifications; a throwback, not to sublime and spiritual suffering, but to the coarse and common pains of earth. Here it is that the true worth of our surrender shall indeed be tested. Here we have the opportunity to prove our love. We are to make an oblation of our very bodies' dignity and reticence: ceding to Him the strong outposts of the citadel of pride. We are to make an oblation of all separateness and selfhood, whether manifested by body, soul, or spirit, to that stern "Acceptor of Sacrifices" who is yet our Father and our Friend.

Should not the growing soul be grateful for these purifying torments here offered to it - for the Scourge, the Thorns, and the Cross? Is it not a part of the unmeasured Divine generosity, that these, the instruments of His Eternal Passion, are freely given to those littlest ones who follow in the way? So much has been given to us; so great a confidence reposed in us, and yet we have fallen so bitterly short of the fullness of the stature of Christ. Surely we are willing to pay for this by a contrition expressed in true penance? - to take our share in "the unimaginable disappointment of God"? Surely needful was this opportunity of pain. Threefold are the roots of imperfection within us. Threefold too must be the purifications wrought in us by these mysteries of sorrow; and here, we stand at the threshold of the first.

The secret ordeal of Gethsemane was but the annunciation of the trials of the adventuring spirit. The life which it elected in that hour of solemn choice is not to be made easy, for it is not, as the Quietists thought, "One Act." Its manhood must be tested in the open, by the mockery, the insults, the unmeaning cruelties of the self-satisfied and imperceptive crowd. With none of the high circumstances of the martyrs - rather as one who has been a nuisance to his kind - the soul goes now to the pillar of utmost self-abasement. There, bound and helpless, exposed in its nakedness to the sharp lashes of earthly opinion, the victim of any who may turn against it - there shall the Christian who lays claim to the mystical fellowship of Jesus first exhibit his generosity, his constancy, his courage: there, down there in the turmoil, the squalor, the hubbub of daily life, where only the man of action is a hero, and the God-intoxicated seer at best a fool.

The whips of the world have always fallen sharply about the limbs of the world's saviours: and each finite soul in whom Christ is brought to birth - who feels the entincturing madness of His heavenly love - participates according to its measure in that great business of salvation; has a part in His redemptive office, helps to fill up the measure of the fullness of God.

We too - though the secret flame within us burns feebly - yet bring to these brothers of ours all that we can tell of the good news of the Kingdom of Reality, the mystery of more abundant life; and most often they meet our exultant tidings with the scourge of their indifference and contempt. We announce to them their royal lineage, and they put upon our head the thorny crown of an insulting tolerance. The helping hands, the willing pilgrim feet are often pierced by them, the self-giving heart is wounded by their scorn. The pains of Christ are felt thus in all His members. They are a veritable part of the pageant of His glory, and only by suffering can we prove our real participation in this His life. A voice comes to us out of the darkness, as we tread the way we think so hard and steep : "O all ye that pass by, behold and see, if there be any sorrow like unto my sorrow." What is your little grief and disappointment beside the sorrow wherewith I am filled? I have loved you with an everlasting love, therefore with loving kindness I have sought you, bringing to your souls the tincture of Eternal Life. I have shown you that life in action, its actual growth towards God. I have not kept my secret to myself. That which I do, I do it in the name of all the race; freely I have received, freely I give. But you have made loneliness my portion; you have cut me off from amongst the sons of men. The bridge that I have built that you might walk thereon, you have deliberately broken down. I would have fed you with My Substance, and you have cast the Bread of Life away. *Ego te pavi manna per desertum; et tu me cecidisti alapis et flagellis.* [10]

It is the voice of the Lord and Lover of men, heard behind the ceaseless noises of the earth-life, sorrowing as He passes amongst us unrecognised and alone. Shall we refuse to follow where He treads? Shall not we too bear on our bodies His livery; receiving for the mystic food we offer the buffet and the scourge? Shall we not elect to stand beside Him, bound to the immovable pillar of the world's prejudice, patient under the pitiless lash of its curiosity, its astonishment, its contempt? Here is our great opportunity of love, great chance of generosity of an actual sharing in the life of God.

"A man once thought," says Tauler, "that God drew some men even by pleasant paths, while others were drawn by the paths of pain. Our Lord answered him thus, 'What think ye can be pleasanter or nobler than to be made most like unto Me? that is by suffering. Mark, to whom was ever offered such a painful and troubled life as to Me? And in whom can I better work, in accordance with My true nobility, than in those who are most like Me? They are the men who suffer. No man ever suffered so bitterly as I; and yet no man was ever so pure as I. When was I more mocked than when I was most glorifying My Heavenly Father? Learn that My Divine Nature never worked so nobly in human nature as by suffering; and because suffering is so efficacious, it is sent out of great love.'"

Yet a mighty exultation, a joy untasted by those who only know the smooth side of the world, waits on the willing sufferer with and for Christ. In the hour of the body's captivity and hardest humiliation, the spirit first knows itself to be free. It lies easily in the hand of God; deliberately it waits upon His Will. With a deep serenity which the condemnation of the world will never trouble - more, with a strange inward joy, a flaming rapture, which the intelligence of the world will never understand - it submits its members to the scourge.

"Who shall separate us," cries Paul, "from the love of Christ? Shall tribulation or distress or persecution or famine or nakedness or peril or sword? Nay! in all these things we are more than conquerors, through Him that loved us!"

More than conquerors: bound to the pillar, enduring the lash of those who believe that they hold us in their power, "nor height nor depth, nor any other creature shall be able to separate us from the love of God." So deeply immersed is the soul in the spiritual universe, so greatly has this harsh call on all its latent manliness increased its stature in that world, that here at the beginning of sorrows it sees itself at the beginning of victories. Its Triumphs are already at hand.

But these mighty declarations bring shame and silence to our little, flickering, self-regarding love, shrinking in terror from collision with the apathy or opposition of the world. They can only be taken on the lips of the great and ardent spirits; the eager chivalry of Christ. The comfortable Christian, snugly wrapped in the decent blankets of tradition; the religious amorist whose secret orchard fulfils all he can demand of Heavenly Love - these cannot pass this way. Here come the true squires of the Eternal Wisdom, following their Master to the lists, that they may prove their loyalty and courage. Here, surrendered to "the sufferings of the time," they are rapt to a foretaste of its glory: they find, mysteriously, a gateway which leads them to the murmurous solitudes of God. There the thud of the descending lash beats time to a celestial music; and the heavenly theme of the soul's symphony, "a melody intolerably sweet," is heard through the crash of the world's discords, moving towards its triumphs in the heights. "Worldly lovers," says Rolle, "soothly words or ditties of our song may know, for the words they read; but the tone and sweetness of that song they may not learn." It is known only by those who go with God to the pillar, submitting to those great rhythms of Creation which beat out, through pain and conflict, the harmony which is Eternal Life.

Third Sorrowful Mystery: The Crown Of Thorns

St Louis brought the Crown of Thorns to Paris, and installed it, with unrecognised appropriateness, in the centre of her seething life; a jewelled symbol of the sovereignty towards which Life, at its best, must ever aspire.

It is the way of humanity to crown its chosen sovereigns with dead things: terrible instruments, wrought with much pain and cunning from the wealth with which it weighs itself down. But when Divine Love broke in on them, those by whom He was despised and rejected did Him, unaware, a greater honour. They took and crowned Him with a diadem torn from the very stuff of life: a diadem possessing life's dreadful qualities of pain and loveliness, of thorns and flowers. They could not give the one without the other: so, all unwittingly they wreathed His brows with beauty whilst they crowned Him with the cruel chaplet of ignominious pain.

Ego dedi tibi sceptrum regale; et tu dedisti capiti meo spineam coronam.[11] Heavy with life, it lay upon His head the imperial crown of humility, won by the agony of the garden and the bitter abasement of the pillar. Even at that hour of coming death, the sap was running in those branches, which seemed so sterile and so hard. The flowery crown of Easter morning is but the thorny crown of Calvary.

The crown of life, then, pressed down upon the brow of life's initiate, is the one great gift the world confers on the growing soul in this dolorous way. Here, in its own despite, it does honour to that Life which it despises and rejects. Paradoxically, as a part of the very process of condemnation, it proclaims the victory of growing Spirit. It feels the sharpness of the thorns that it inflicts, and rejoices in them: but the budding roses in their axils it cannot see.

> ' "They wove for me a crown of truth, and it caused
> Thy branches to bud in me,
> For it is not like a withered crown which buddeth not:
> But Thou livest upon my head, and Thou hast
> blossomed upon my head.
> Thy fruits are full grown and perfect; they are full of
> Thy salvation."

"It caused Thy branches to bud in me!" Still the mystery of growth is with the soul, governing its experience even in this dark hour, working in it the wonderful paradox of tribulation, the upspringing of life and beauty beneath the burden of failure and grief. "It is not like a withered crown. . . . Thou livest upon my head." His abounding life dispensed under the strangest of disguises; His benediction resting on the very instruments of most bitter mortification, and making of them the dearest gifts of love.

He demanded of us the subjection of our physical life, the surrender of the body's dignity and power to the purposes of ascending spirit; and according to our self-giving power we gave it. Now, the regnant mind, the piercing intellect that probed the world's secrets, the quick imagination that ran before our feet to look upon the secrets of His love - these dearest qualities of ours, that we wished only to dedicate to His service, to remake in the interests of His life, He takes, as it seems, that He may break and degrade them before the amused and malicious eyes of other men. We must be fools, glad fools, for Christ's sake: all has been given us, and all we must give again. So, after the outward indignity of the scourging the soul must face that more subtle torture, the mockery of the royal crown: the world's most poignant criticism, the act by which it marks its sense of spirit's strangeness and separation - the wild arrogance, as it seems, of its pretensions, the irrational absurdity of its dreams. We offer the world our love, and it repays us with a pretended reverence bowing the knee whilst it steels the heart. It is not ashamed to find immortal spirit "interesting," even in the hour in which it consigns it to the Cross.

Yet against its will, as it were, the world helps the work which must be done within us. It, too, is an instrument held in the sure and skilful hand of God. It is teaching us the "gymnastic of Eternity," the high lessons of the School of Perfect Resignation making plain the way on which we are to travel, bringing us the only food that can nourish and support our stormy love.

> ' "Bring thorns for the path of the enthusiast,
> His love would have them daggers" -

and it makes them as sharp as it can, barbs them with ridicule, little knowing that the wounds which they inflict are the secret pathways by which His love and grace come in: or that the dreadful wreath into which they are platted is the ensign of the soul's eternal sovereignty.

"Christ hath crowned me," said St Agnes in the brothel, "with the bright and priceless blossoms of the Eternal Spring" - sweet radiance, purity, and fruitfulness, His beauty perpetually upspringing, given out of the deeps of bodily degradation for the adornment of the virgin soul. As those who run in the games for a perishable garland, so we have brought our body into subjection, have sought even at the pillar the harsh discipline of the spiritual athlete; that we may win an imperishable crown. Now at last it is given us; not under circumstance of outward triumph, but so as our victory may seem to the world defeat.

"From glory to glory advancing, we praise Thee, the Saviour of Souls," as we go from garden to pillar, from the judgment-hall to the cross. We tread a primrose path, though our eyes are holden: we grow up into the fullness of His stature, our weakness the very condition of His strength. Whether it be the slow process of nature or the deliberate art of man to which we are submitted, "all serveth," says Boehme, "but abundantly to manifest the wonderful works of God, that He for all and in all may be glorified. Yea, all serveth if thou knowest rightly how to use it, only to recollect thee more inwards, and to draw thy spirit into that majestic Light wherein the original patterns and forms of things visible are to be seen. Keep therefore in the Centre, and stir not from the Presence of God revealed within thy soul."

In the Light which fills that secret place is laid up for us the pattern of our imperishable Crown. It is made of roses, wild and fragrant, and "in each rose is written the word Love." To that centre we may retreat, though the world clamour about us, to offer Him the fruits of our surrender, made manifest in pain. What else indeed is there that we can give, from our poor little treasure-house, so nearly worthy of His acceptance as this? How else could we exhibit the heroic quality of our love? In the deep silence of the growing garden, our wills were made over to His Will, in the judgment-hall of human opinion, our bodies were submitted to the scourge - yes, to anything that might befall them; worse, the purple robe of an inglorious honour was set about our shoulders by those who will never understand. Now, the head made bare for His unction receives the thorny crown, and with it a new and deeper participation in the eternal passion of His Christ. Man's dearest pride, the instrument of his deep thought and piercing vision, the citadel of his power; the secret garden as he fancies, where alone he has rapt communion with his dream - this must taste the humiliation which is more bitter than the pangs of death.

Bit by bit, the Whole Man is to be brought within the magic ring of suffering. The totality of human nature, Body, Soul, and Spirit, must be welded together in the likeness of the humiliation of Christ; that we may follow in His footsteps on the dolorous way which leads to the Father's heart. The Salt, the Sulphur, and the Mercury - all must be cast into pain's crucible. There the fire of love shall transmute them into the substance of Spiritual Gold.

> *"Love not too much.' But how,*
> *When Thou hast made me such,*
> *And dost Thy gifts bestow,*
> *How can I love too much?*
> *Though I must fear to lose,*
> *And drown my joy in care,*
> *With all its thorns I choose*
> *The path of love and prayer."*

Fourth Sorrowful Mystery: The Bearing Of The Cross

When the chivalry of the squire has been tested he may ride with his Lord in the lists. When the education of the climber has prospered, he may set his face towards the hills. So, disciplined in mind and body by the cruelest oppositions which the world of things can offer, pilgrim man must now prepare to leave that world behind him: set out upon his long viaticum of ascent. "The Love of God," says Angela of Foligno, "is never idle; for it constrains us to follow the Way of the Cross." Pressing in on us, transfusing us, encompassing us as an atmosphere, thrusting Life forward on its long quest of Perfection, that stern and tender love compels its children to the only journey which leads home. It blocks all other paths - so easy and so tempting for us - the way of knowledge, the way of beauty, even the way of human goodness with the rest. The enticement and the pursuit, the companionship and the loneliness, the light and the shadow of the Divine Desire all these in their interplay force us to one narrow, peopled path; a path of unutterable harshness that leads as it seems to the place of death, yet shall lead us if we trust it to the only country of the soul.

The pilgrimage to Calvary is the third stage in Life's long drama of self-giving; the self-giving upon which the soul resolved when it came forth from the Garden of Prayer. Since we are "made-trinity, like to the unmade blissful Trinity," three-fold must be our self-yielding to its love. "Man," says Tauler, "is just as though he were formed of three men; his animal nature, in which he is guided by his senses; his powers of reason; and his highest nature, which is in the image and likeness of God." We have left our sensual nature bound to the pillar. Itself a captive, we have no more to fear from its assaults. Our reason we have submitted to that thorny crown of humiliation, which waits for every initiate of the Sorrowful Mysteries of Christ. Now, we must leave both behind us; and, ascending "above reason and beyond reason," "go up alone with the Son into the secret place, the Holy of Holies," that we may offer our utmost sacrifice, that is, our very selves, and enter in, "hiding the secret mind in the mystery of the Divine Abyss." Even whilst the spirit sorrows beneath its burden, it knows that it is going to its Love; that this is the only way to perfect union with the Godhead, the veritable thoroughfare of life. "What ask I of thee more, but that thou study to resign thyself to Me entirely? What thing soever thou givest Me else I care not for."

We stretched our hearts and minds towards Him, blind yet

desirous; growing, as we hoped, gently yet from glory to glory in His image, striving towards the fullness of the stature of Christ. Now we begin to feel in its irresistible power the pull of His terrible attraction. Steadily, remorselessly, it draws us along the cruel road that seems to lead to the spiritual death. The Voice says again: "As nothing should suffice thee without Me, likewise nothing may please Me whatsoever thou shalt give, if thou offer not thyself to Me." And we, full of fear yet full of adoration, go forward step by step, driven by that all-conquering impulse; by God without Who calls to God within. His attraction it is that compels us, yet we think that we do it ourselves: as the crumb of steel caught within the magnetic area may congratulate itself upon the swiftness with which it runs to its appointed and inevitable place.

"And all this," says Julian, Diotima of the Symposium of Christ's lovers, "showed He full blissfully, signifying thus:

"See! I am God: see! I am in all thing: see! I do all thing; see! I lift never mine hands off my works, nor ever shall, without end: see! I lead all thing to the end I ordained it to from without beginning, by the same Might, Wisdom, and Love whereby I made it. How should anything be amiss?"

How indeed should anything be amiss with the soul which is brought to birth in Him? Even on the Sorrowful Way, in manifold failures and humiliations, it lives and moves and has its being within the charmed circle of His grace. Men think that it suffers hell, yet it stands in heaven for it knows, in the midst of squalor and of anguish, in the midst of its struggles and its falls, that His hands are never lifted from His works. Thus He shapes and thus transmutes us: slowly distilling the perdurable tincture of Eternity from the crude and unenduring stuff of time. This is His way: and shall we ask another? "Dost thou think to escape what never mortal man might escape? What saint in this world was without cross and tribulation?"

As the joyful mystery of the Visitation, so is the mystery of this slow and bitter climb to death. It is a way of prayer: a mystical ascent to new and close communion with our Master, along the least promising of paths. It is a plumbing of all experience, even the terrible experience of spiritual failure, that we may seek and find Him in the very deeps. It is a way of dark contemplation; for we move as it were in His shadow, yet cannot see Him at our side. We go in great solitude; though the populations of the earth are close about us, and the populations of Eternity are surely there to bless. Out of the midst of our hard climbing, the slow, difficult course - the dust, the heat, the burden, only actual to us - we look as from an infinite distance, at the world we have known so well. Yet our path lies through that world. The Holy Mountain we are climbing rises amongst its tenements and streets; and its inhabitants come out to us as we struggle up the steep monotonous pathway, to urge, to help, to grieve. Strange adventures befall us as we plod upwards. Not pain and effort alone shall be our portion. We go through the midst of life; it flows about us, presses upon our consciousness in every shape and form. Sweet human Love meets us; and we turn from her imploring eyes with terror, for she must not withhold us from our destiny. Wayfaring Love meets us, plain and homely; and eases, as none other can, the cruel burden of the Cross. Intuitive Love runs to our encounter, ministers to us in our distress; mysteriously discerning in our features, distorted though they be with weariness and anguish, the Veritable Image of its Friend. The amateurs of Religious Sentiment meet us; and perhaps their facile pity is the hardest thing the soul has got to bear. They are interested in its struggle, and follow for a little way, stepping delicately to avoid the mud and stones but they deplore the ill-regulated enthusiasm which has led to this piteous pass. Religion, they think, should be calm, sweet, and beautiful; the way that leads to God should be run without dust or heat. They will go home, to weep over their pretty pious books, kneeling upon their comfortable hassocks; safe as it were in a respectable and stagnant backwater, far from those raging torrents which pour towards the Infinite Sea.

As for the soul brought to this bitter mystery, all its love and will, all its strength and endurance, must now be set upon one point. Desire and thought shall sink almost into abeyance; so central for its consciousness must be the passionate effort, the tense determination to bear all things "according to His will." Bit by bit it must struggle upwards, slipping, falling; its manliness is being tested here if ever, under the crushing burden of the saving Cross. The shadow of that Cross lies for it upon Creation, a term which delimits without error the kingdoms of the unreal and the real. "Behold! in the Cross all doth consist." It dominates the lover's consciousness, and reduces all else that cannot live within its radiance to the ranks of the shadowy and the insecure. To bear it, is to bear His primal secret with us; the merciless touchstone of truth, strong even in our utmost weakness. The phantoms fly before it all the pious fancies, all the ethical pretensions, all the philosophic dreams. "For the word of the Cross is to them that are perishing foolishness; but to us that are being saved it is the Power of God" - His Wisdom in a mystery, declaring in inexorable, sternest action that deepest secret of the universe which shall never be communicated in words. "One desire only," says St John of the Cross, "does God allow and suffer in His Presence: that of perfectly observing His law, and of carrying the Cross of Christ. In the Ark of the Covenant there was but the Book of the Law, the Rod of Aaron, the Pot of Manna. Even so that soul which has no other aim than the perfect observance of the Law of God, and the carrying of the Cross of Christ, will be a true Ark containing the true Manna, which is God."

Fifth Sorrowful Mystery: The Crucifixion

Under pressure of its inward impulse to transcendence, that steadfast tendency to deity which nothing can withstand, the pilgrim soul is come to a most still, bare, and desolate place; where it seems that nothing lives but God alone. That achievement of Reality for which it asked, towards which indeed its whole growth has been directed, is at last accomplished in it. The veils of illusion are torn away. Every member is pierced by the wound of Perfect Love, and it is lifted up from the earth into the lonely desert of the Godhead - lifted up upon the saving Cross. Merciless hands have stripped the I, the Me, the Mine, from it; those decent garments which shrouded the immortal personality within, sheltered its limbs from the sharp air of the supernal sphere. Only the naked spirit in its hour of utmost destitution comes to this altar, and in perfect self-abandonment sets foot upon this ladder to the stars.

> *"This is Love! to fly heavenward,*
> *To rend, every instant, a hundred veils.*
> *The first moment, to renounce life;*
> *The last step, to fare without feet."*

It is not the consummation towards which spirit had looked at the beginning of its journey: that Divine Manhood, that wholeness of life perfected and completed in Him, toward which the regenerate soul, it thought, should grow. But now that soul has learned that love is enough for it, and that only in the extreme of surrender can love have its perfect work. Like some homing star which has burned its way swifter and ever swifter to the sphere that called it, purged and made shining by the ardour of its flight, it rushes through the shrouding darkness to its Origin. All its desire now is to be lost in Him. It thinks no more of its own transcendence; of its little separate achievement, its spirituality, its pain. Only it wants to "go forward, and get nearer to the Eternal Goodness" if it can. By effort and sacrifice it would do it, for its love is vital, and wears the colours of chivalry and romance. It asks for difficulties; for opportunity of endurance. In the end no smoother way could have been bearable to it than the Royal Highway of the Cross. The choice, the effort, the self-stripping, the purging and transmuting fires - even the darkness, desolation, and abandonment, the bitterness of the spiritual death - were they not needed, the soul had almost demanded them, that thus it might test for Him its courage and its faith. Here is the true blessedness of spirit's imprisonment in the body, its submission to the imperfections and limitations of the flesh; that so by heroic effort, by the heavenly romance of self-donation, it might win its way to freedom; working out its salvation in fear and trembling, yet in the joyous exercise of industrious and courageous love, till the Eternal Christ is disclosed in the fullness of His beauty and His power.

O certe necessarium Adæ peccatum, quod Christi morte deletum est! O felix culpa, quæ talem ac tantum meruit habere redemptorem! [12]

Dear, happy fault, which gave us something to do for Him; oh, deepest secret of divinest music, the disharmony which had to be resolved.

Compelled to the gesture of a boundless generosity, its arms outstretched to the embrace of all things - the evil and the lovely, the clean and the unclean - its heart made wider by the wound which pierced it, thereby to make space for the entrance of His all-demanding love - here it is that the fullness of Creative Energy seizes upon the finite human creature; here at last is consummated the spiritual marriage of the soul. Long time the Love without has called to Love within; but the ramparts of the sense-life must be broken before their mysterious transfusion can take place. A perfect abjection and a total self-spending are asked, as the price of our union with God. Christ Himself showed us this pathway; and declared to us the paradox of life upspringing from corruption and death. He, the supremely Real, trod first for us this difficult bridge which spans the gulf between Appearance and Reality, and leads from a dying world to the heart of intensest life. Paul, following in His footsteps, turned back his transfigured countenance to cry to us, "Dying, and behold I live! God forbid that I should glory save in the Cross."

Here the Body and Blood of God were broken and spilt for us; not alone the bodily expression, the manifestation in Time, but the Spirit of Life itself, "the blood which is the life thereof," He gave. That pouring out of the Precious Blood, the Divine Life, upon the cross of suffering, renewed on every altar, experienced afresh by every soul that comes face to face with Reality, has ever been discerned by Christians as the condition of salvation for the individual and the race. Life itself was then given - "more abundant life" for the world - a fresh dower of vitality, to stimulate the languid soul to new creative acts.

Accipiens et hunc præclarum Calicem in sanctas ac venerabiles manus suas; item tibi gratias agens benedixit, deditque discipulis suis, dicens: Accipite et bibite ex eo omnes. Hic est enim Calix Sanguinis mei, novi et æterni testamenti; mysterium fidei; qui pro vobis et pro multis effundetur in remissionem peccatorum. Hæc quotiescumque feceritis, in mei memoriam facietis. [13]

Do this in renewal of My memory, following in the footsteps of life. Give as I have given; freely ye have received, freely give. All - body, soul, and spirit - is asked of you: a complete offering upon the great altar of the world. In your own interest I ask it: do, that you may know. Nothing can explain to us the mystery of Love and Pain but a sharing of it. Nothing can initiate us into the Life of God which is our peace, if we turn from the cleaving sword of sacrifice and outstretched arms which make up the everlasting mercy of the Cross. The first for rebellious matter, the second for homeward-rushing spirit. Both for Man and Man only - freely offered to him - the instruments of his deification, the signs of a veritable partaking of the life of Christ.

"For He desires," says Ruysbroeck, with the strange and violent imagery of the great mystic who is struggling to describe an intuition which transcends the resources of speech, "He desires to consume our very life, in order that He may change it into His own. . . . Were our eyes keen enough to see this the avid appetite of Christ, Who hungers for our salvation, all our efforts could not keep us from flying to His open mouth. I seem to speak follies; but all who love will understand. For the love of Jesus is of a noble nature. That which He devours He would feed. When He has utterly devoured us, then it is that He gives Himself to us: and endows us with an eternal hunger and thirst."

"He brought me to the banqueting house, and His banner over me was love." Yes, but it seems to the fastidious earthly appetite, the feeble, shrinking human creature, that harshest bread and bitter herbs are the matter of this marriage feast; and the narrow bed of the Cross is cruel to those whose members are unmortified. The soul is held there transfixed in the gathering darkness, enduring the terrible assaults of His grace, the agonies of His initiatory caress, "consumed yet quickened by the glance of God." The dark hours pass, yet it seems that dawn will never come. But even in its despair the loving soul is glad to give itself, for since He asks it, who could demand a better fate?

"I understood," says Julian of this august experience, "that we be now, in our Lord's meaning, in His Cross with Him in His pains and His passion, dying; and we, willingly abiding in the same Cross with His help and His grace unto the last point, suddenly He shall change His cheer to us, and we shall be with Him in heaven. Betwixt that one and the other shall be no time, and then shall all be brought to joy."

"All shall be brought to joy." The fire of love at last shall do its perfect work in us; in the twinkling of an eye we shall be changed. The mystics, casting about for metaphors that shall hint at these strange adventures of the spirit, say that the soul endures upon the Cross not the pains of death but the travail of yet another birth - a difficult, slow birth, that brings it into the steady radiance of a diviner day. It comes forth from the sheltering womb of nature, in which it has lain so warm, so safe, so blind. The last traces of the earth-life pass from it in its agony: all those unrealities, all those checks upon its truest freedom, which it thought essential to its joy. They are going: and in their wake there go at last the dark night, the loneliness and the horror, expressions one and all of a charity as yet imperfect, which dared not all to hope nor all endure. The dawn comes, and peace with it - the day breaks, shadows flee from us; and all at last is brought to blessedness.

> ' "Passing away, saith my God, passing away;
> Winter passeth after the long delay:
> New grapes on the vine, new figs on the tender spray.
> Turtle calleth turtle in Heaven's May.
> Though I tarry, wait for Me, trust Me, watch and pray.
> Arise, come away, night is past, and lo, it is day,
> My love, My sister, My spouse, thou shalt hear Me say.
> Then I answered: Yea."

The Triumphant Mysteries of the Soul's Ascent

First Triumphant Mystery: The Resurrection

Out of that healing darkness in which the soul was lost on Calvary, there steals upon its vision "like a child from the womb, like a ghost from the tomb," the radiant form of a new transfigured life in which it is to share. Gently that life comes forth from the very heart of Earth our Mother: "not with observation," not with the sudden effulgence of the lightning flashing from east to west, but with the mild unhurried majesty of dawn. "Awake, thou that sleepest, arise from the dead, and Christ shall give thee light." The flooding tide of His Divine life invades the finite thing reborn in Him, filling to the brim the emptied channels of its surrendered selfhood, blessing with a new vitality its every faculty and deed: and suddenly in an ecstasy of joy and wonder it knows itself a veritable "partaker of the Divine Nature," remade in Him, "in another form, another glory, another power."

The soul comes from the dereliction and self-naughting of Calvary - from that unimaginable darkness of mind and loneliness of heart - into the world of the Risen Christ: into that everlasting Easter-fact, the Kingdom of Reality ablaze with God, which here and now awaits us. "And after long woe, suddenly our eyes shall be opened, and in clearness of light our sight shall be full." The Angel who met Mary upon Carmel, *Dominus tecum* on his lips: the Angel who was with the soul in its agony, and ministered to it of the Chalice of the Will: the Angel who loves and tends all growing, striving things - he comes once more to initiate the Christian into this new, last stage of his long pilgrimage. Very early in the morning, as the blessed night, *in quæ terrenis cælestia, humanis divina junguntur,*[14] fades away, he shall

104

roll back the heavy stone that shut us in that Cave of Illusion, the sepulchre of the earthly imagination. Then we, amazed and exultant, shall come out to see before us a world renewed and yet the same: lit by that new colour known of those who see Creation with the eyes of God. The winter is past, the rain is over and gone; the flowers appear on the earth; the time of the singing of birds is come. The birthpangs of death have done their work. All was then demanded of the soul; its faith, hope, love, fused in one superhuman act of resignation. It gave all, and gladly since He asked it; stripped-itself of everything but pain. Now all is restored, full measure and pressed down. Because it gave its life to Him it shall now receive the mighty dower of His vitality. Because it was not afraid to enter His darkness, lit only by the faint lantern of humble and self-giving love, now it is inundated with the Uncreated Light. As it believed, it poured out for Him its very life-blood: and lo! there is ichor in its veins. Joy it renounced for Him; and now it is filled with a wild happiness, the mighty exultation of the Sons of God.

For every soul that follows in His footsteps, that elects the heroic vocation of surrender - the scourge, the rosy crown, the heavy cross - the Easter Garden waits at the end of sorrows, fragrant with unimaginable perfumes, and made lovely with the simplest growing things. Here and now, it stretches out beyond our earthy sepulchre, athwart the teeming streets and huddled houses that seem to shut us from the light. Christ walks in it: and behold! not all the cohorts of His Father's angels mark His presence, but hedge and coppice breaking into flower. Suddenly from the tomb where our separated life was laid away, we shall come out into that world, so real and so supernal. Shy and astonished, we shall move with tentative footsteps upon its kindly turf.

"I was glad when they said unto me, Let us go into the House of the Lord." Green-meshed are the airy vaults of it, and violet-blue its cool and shaded floor. The innocent furred acolytes of His Mysteries go without fear between its aisles; the birds and angels sit together in its trees. A Gardener moves between those borders, and blossoms spring between His wounded feet. New life He radiates, and not alone on human spirits. All Creation waits upon His coming; and where He passes by He brings it peace.

Here at last His veritable encounter is made possible to us: here the deepest secrets of His Love are declared to us under the simplest accidents of natural life. "My beloved is mine, and I am His: He feedeth among the lilies." As the veil that hangs before the Tabernacle, so do these dew-drenched branches, so does this heavenly inflorescence, shroud the gateway to the Garden of His joy. "My secret to myself": once more for a space the soul is alone with it; alone with the whispered messages of morning, the hushed ecstasies of life. Only the radiant wounds that bless its members remind it of the torments of the past. "In the House of its Friend" it received them. This at last it knows, and knowing, does not seek to understand: for now it is "one thing with Him," buried with Him, risen with Him - at last its life is hidden with Christ in God. Human love comes to meet it; but in this rapt and sacred hour the soul must cry, "Touch me not," for another contact is about its limbs. God enfolds it as an atmosphere: it stands on earth, and yet it lives in heaven.

What, then, is it to mean for us, this Resurrection-life of the transfigured soul, remade upon the levels of Reality? What did it mean for our Master, in the matchless hour of His return, when He walked the solitary garden and communed with its still and fragrant life? It meant a coming back to earth of that deified spirit which was caught into the arms of God in its utmost surrender: a deliberate reversion, in the fullness of its power, in the ardour of its burning charity, to the plane of the shadowy, the imperfect, the unreal. It meant the beginning of the Eternal Return which the Holy Eucharist makes actual to us; a self-spending, a giving of Himself under the humblest limitations, that He may be food for the very life of men. This it is that makes us certain of the perfection of Christ's union with the Father - not His ineffable immersion in that Divine Reality, but His sweet and steady care for littlest human interests, the undistorted love which led Him to transfigure with His presence the poor diurnal life of common things. He does not disdain to entice with gentlest intimacies our reluctant faith and trust. He comes into our midst and shows to us the wounds on His creative hands, His untiring feet; even the way that leads to His sacred heart. We find Him in the solitary mountain. He stands among us on the shore. He is a Guest at our table, and ministers to us the hidden manna, the very substance of His life. He accepts even the fruits of our poor labours - gentlest of all the courtesies of God. Not for His own sake, but for the sake of humanity He returns to us; returns to the patient earth, His mother and ours. There in the early morning He comes to meet us, bearing that banner of our redemption which is the ensign of His triumph and our hope; proof that the Pathfinder has found a way. There He nests in the heart of life and waits our search of Him, waits till he can again come to birth in the arid and reluctant human soul.

> ' "Tell us where the Lord sojourneth,
> For we find an empty tomb.
> Whence He sprung, there He returneth,
> Mystic Sun, the Virgin's womb.
> Hidden Sun, His beams so near us,
> Cloud-empillared as He was,
> From of old there He, Ischyros,
> Waits our search, Athanatos."

It is the dearest ambition of the Christian, the final evidence of consecrated love, that the Easter-fact may be manifest in him also, even under the veils and limitations of the flesh. He too would live in the interests of humanity the transfigured life in the here-and-now. Since there dwells in his heart the very presence of the Strong and the Immortal, he desires that this strength and immortality may be his own, to spend for other men.

Surely here the desire of man encounters the desire of God which runs to meet it. From the Easter-fact, transcendent life is indeed poured out on us, to take and make our own and spend again. It streams upon us from the altar: it meets us in the silence of the hills; it buds mysteriously within the soul. Yet not for our own sakes is it given us; rather that we may follow in the steps of our Pattern, and go back to entincture with new gold the desirous world of men. For love's sake we shall return to them, in their midst our true, completed life shall be manifest; here, not in some far-off region of the "spiritual," begin the triumphant mysteries of His Grace. "Awake, O north wind; and come, thou south, blow upon my garden, that the spices thereof may flow out." They shall flow out into the sad and sterile tracts of earth, to heal, to fertilise, to make fragrant, giving news of the secret place from which they come: the heavenly garden, everywhere awaiting us, where Love and Wisdom meet in the heart of the Living God.

Second Triumphant Mystery: The Ascension

The life of the regenerate spirit - that Christ-like thing which agonised and died, that it might rise within the soul to greater glory - is like a well of living water perpetually uprising, pouring itself out in diurnal acts of benediction towards men.

It cannot fade or tire, it cannot fluctuate; for the deep springs of its being are fed perpetually by the fontal and exuberant Life of God. It moves in a transfigured world, it touches all things to fresh power and loveliness; endows them with its sacramental life.

Yet this, its royal new approach to things created, has at once its counterpart and its origin in a new approach now made possible for it towards the uncreated sphere. Not of its own strength, but because of its eternal attachments made perfect, its mighty outward swing to the Unseen, does it live the risen life within the world; because of the consummation of that union to which the discipline of prayer has slowly led. Hence it is natural that this same growing life of prayer, the heavenly correspondence which alone supports and makes possible the fruitful correspondences of earth, should demand its own expression, a space made clear for its peculiar activities, within the circle of the transfigured life.

Bit by bit, yet very gently, we are led into all the wonders of that new existence. So great is the reverence of our Lover for the littleness and ignorance of the soul, so matchless the humility of God, that He chooses to await the slow discovery of that spirit whom he has made only for Himself. His companionship waits ever at the margin of the mind. But that mind must turn to Him if it would know all the splendours of communion: going up with the sharp dart of longing love from the created to the uncreated sphere. This act, the act of prayer made perfect, has now become for it the highest of all arts, the Science of all Sciences, the Romance in which all longings are fulfilled. So we need not be astonished that the passion for the Real often seizes upon the soul, rapturously and suddenly: abruptly inducts the citizen into the Heavenly Country, catches him from the earth and inundates him with the Uncreated Light. In swift ascents of joy his love will go out toward that Love of God which rushes in to meet it: that so the Loved and Lover may at last be made "one thing."

> ' "In a place beyond uttermost Place, in a track
> without shadow of trace,
> Soul and body transcended, I live in the soul of
> my Loved One anew!"

Such is the experience of the soul's true ecstasy; such the Ascension which it makes to the Father, as the pioneer of growing mounting life. Like a bird, says St Gregory, was the ascent of our Forerunner, swiftly and easily borne upward on the feathers of fine love "and the path of that Bird knoweth no man, who believeth not in the ascension into heaven."

This is the third of Love's mysterious ascents towards Reality; the third journey of that insatiable adventurer up the Mountain of Contemplation. The first time, it went on an errand of courtesy bearing the seed of a life as yet unborn; and its prayer was the prayer of simplicity, a glad confession of joy and faith. The second time it went on an errand of sacrifice, bearing the cruel burden of the Cross; and its prayer was an act of pure surrender to the Will. Now, for the last time, it goes up in triumph, free, unfettered: and its prayer is the ecstatic upward rush of the winged spirit, borne by its simplicity and its purity made perfect to immediate union with the Heart of God.

"A man," says Thomas à Kempis, "is lifted up from earthly things with two wings: they are simplicity and purity. Simplicity ought to be in intention; purity in affection. Simplicity intendeth God, purity taketh Him and tasteth Him."

Simplicity, that is singleness of eye, looks upon God; sees Him in all and above all, the one Transcendent Fact of many facets, outside of Whom is no existence, and in Whom is no darkness at all. Purity, that is singleness of heart, receives and tastes Him; undistracted by any conflict of desires. On these two wings the spirit, remade in Christ, takes flight toward the Eternal, to that superessential Being in which all life has its beginning and its end; there to enjoy as the term of its difficult ascents a veritable fruition of the Absolute.

"He hath set His Beauty above the stars: His loveliness is in the clouds of heaven." Only by a forsaking and overpassing of the earth-life can we truly know it: by a lifting up of the heart towards its home. Not the unresting and immanent Love that works and watches within the framework of the here-and-now, but an utterly transcendent Truth and Beauty, which alone may satisfy our craving, calls us upwards. We are drawn to some unspeakable region, to some imageless experience, where, on the pivot of all time and space, our hunger and thirst for God shall at last be stilled. "This deification and elevation of the spirit in God," says St John of the Cross, "whereby the soul is, as it were rapt and absorbed in love, made one with God, suffers it not to dwell upon any worldly matter. The soul is now detached, not only from all outward things, but even from itself: it is, as it were, undone, assumed by, and dissolved in, Love. The which is to say, that it passes out of itself into the Beloved."

"*Into* the beloved" - into the Ocean of Godhead, into the Fathomless Abyss. Thither He was caught up from the summits of contemplation; "And a cloud received Him out of their sight." No human eye shall look upon that joyous consummation no human mind shall penetrate the wonder of the mystic's ecstasy. If we go up with Jesus to the high summit of our spirit, to the mountain of the imageless fact, if we follow Him with the rapt gaze of simplicity, with that intimate and eager comradeship, up the steep slopes of our ascending love; then, led of Him, in Him, through Him, our veritable ascension may be accomplished - that paradoxical ascension of the Christian consciousness, which is really the humblest of descents. "To be immersed in humility is to be immersed in God." This is the triumph of complete self-loss, when at last the soul can say with Catherine, "My Me is God, nor do I know my self-hood out of Him." Then we, not knowing what befalls us, deep hidden in the Cloud of Unknowing, shall indeed for one unspeakable and transient moment "meet the Lord in the air." Then it is that exultant joy shall have its perfect work in us; snatching us from the tame fields of the "reasonable" and enfolding us in that radiant darkness which hides the supremely happy from the sight of other men.

Those other men, so wistful and so eager, long to understand, if they may not experience, these strange and wild adventures of the soul. But the spiritual marriage is not to be accomplished before the astonished eyes of the looker-on. This is the dearest secret of supremest love: and He is a "bashful lover, that His sweetheart before men entreats not." Darkness was on Calvary when first the spirit felt His "terrible initiatory caress." Now in the hour of its ecstatic union a shining cloud receives it, dark with excess of light. It knows not where it may be, for every landmark is transcended: giving and receiving have become for it meaningless and unintelligible words. It has passed from contemplation to fruition: is immersed as for the time of its ecstasy in the silent music and the murmurous solitude of God. In that swift act of spiritual union, that brief immersion in Eternity, He communicates to the soul Life, Knowledge, and Beatitude then all is consummated, all is renewed. Baptized into the embraces of Love, above all reason, above all knowledge, only under the veils of highest poetry can it report to us the faint outline of its wonder and its joy.

Third Triumphant Mystery: The Coming of the Holy Spirit

The mysteries of the Ascension and of Pentecost, taken together, may well represent to us the necessary double action of the complete and wholly conscious human spirit: its solitary and prayerful ascents to God, its eager and outflowing activity towards the world of men. "The possession of God," says Ruysbroeck, "demands and supposes a perpetual activity": each upward rush towards communion with His Perfect Beauty involves a return to the restless and imperfect world of Becoming, a sharing in the creative industries of His Immanent Love.

There have been mystics who fancied that the ecstatic ascent to Pure Being, that *Mentis alienatio* which seemed to Richard of St Victor the perfect consummation of all prayer, was the end of the soul's career. They held that those whom Beatrice led up the Celestial Ladder were not destined to come down again; thus passing a sentence of sterility upon the spiritual marriage of the soul. But the true ecstasy of the contemplative snatched up to fruition of God is an ascent undertaken in the interests of humanity, even as our Forerunner ascended in order that "the Paraclete might come." Every Christian soul is brother to Prometheus, and seeks the heavenly fire, not for his own glory but because he must transmit it to the race. He is a thoroughfare: a completed self, but not, for that very reason, self-sufficing: doubly dependent, rather, on the vivifying grace that he receives and on the eager service that he gives. Thus the ascension into heaven was but the opening episode of Divine Humanity's true and eternal activities: the condition of that fecundity, that unexhaustible self-spending, that power of spiritual creation, proper to a life which is fulfilled of God. He that has made ascensions to the Father, let the proof of his transcendence be a humble and willing return to the sphere of illusion, as a part of that great spiritual chivalry, that knighthood of the Paraclete, which defends and guides and strengthens life on its upward path.

There is here then no selfish abstraction from the actual, no deliberate neglect of the lovely life of service which is Christ's; but one-half of the completed self-expression of man in his wholeness, that citizen of time and of Eternity, "swinging between the Unseen and the Seen." The transfigured life, the new universe to which he has been lifted, the One by Whom that life and universe are filled, demand of the new man a wholeness of response: a world-renouncing response to Love Transcendent ever enticing him, a world-accepting response to Love Immanent, which ever calls him to share and to comfort the pain and weakness of created things. Humblest charity, highest contemplation: these are the facets of that crystal which shall reflect the Inaccessible Light.

But these difficult responses to Finite and to Infinite shall and must depend on a constant renewal and refreshing; on a contact with the Transcendent "never to be lost or broken," on a conscious self-mergence of the soul "as a fish in the sea, as a bird in the air," in the Infinite Being of God. They shall depend on the soul's continual nurture by His feeding and inflowing Grace: given in the days of our weakness as dew upon the tender grass, and in the stormy times of our adolescence as the drenching vivifying showers; now sweeping as a mighty wind through the airy kingdoms of the spirit, and blessing, fertilising, where it goes.

Jacob Boehme, that deep gazer into the secrets of God, has somewhere a mysterious saying about the "Outflown Word": an image, as it were, of the Divine Wisdom rushing out as a great wind from its own centre and passing through the meshes of the Cosmos, a swift and searching tempest of life. That wind blows where it lists, filling with its sound the whole world of Becoming; sometimes a storm of inspiration, sometimes a murmurous and refreshing breeze. Earth treads her cyclic path about the floor of heaven enfolded in the music of its gale. It stirs in all natural things and compels them to a manifestation of its beauty. It collects and it scatters. It enables and it slays. It moves the souls of men who know it not, evoking in them diversities of gifts.

The winds of the world in their passage move to new and various qualities of loveliness each living thing they touch. They toss the great boughs into the air and fill them with a wild and passionate delight. They dapple with delicate and shaded glories the surface of the fields. They stir the grave wheat to measured rhythms, make a fringed mystery of the barley, give to the oats a delicate playfulness, an elfin quality of life. They drive the cloudy castles over the long savannahs of the blue. Everywhere they inspire change, life, movement; forcing the sap upwards through the living, swaying branches, shaking the fertile pollen from the flowers, stirring thought and passion, giving beauty for ashes, music for silence, energising enthusiastically in the interests of Eternal Wisdom and Eternal Joy.

"As the hand moves over the harp and the strings speak, so speaks in my members the Spirit of the Lord, and I speak by His Love."

The psalm of that perpetual adoration can be heard of all in sea and forest. No less, in the angels' ears, its acceptable melody may be discerned in the home and cloister, in the studio, the workshop, and the shrine. To some participation in this angelic awareness of the Wind of God our new life must introduce us: to a natural and active world, swept everywhere by those untamed and vital breezes - a world that is in all its activities inspired.

This new and unifying consciousness of Spirit, comes to us from without; completing for us the Trinity in Unity of a reality that is and must be conterminous with God. In the joys of the spiritual childhood we have known His care and protection as a Father. In a sharing of His sufferings and His efforts, we have known the travail of the Son. Now in our maturity we know Him as Omnipresent Spirit, the one Reality of all that is: and we ask for the fullness of that Spirit to be upon us, that we may live with the full span of its immortal and creative life.

> *"Wild Spirit which art moving everywhere,*
> *Destroyer and Preserver, hear, O hear!"*

And our prayer is answered, since it is made in lowliness of heart. Suddenly His life is amongst us in its fullness. It penetrates the world of things, and lights on us as we sit amongst our kind. As flaming fire, as rushing wind, it seems to us in its power and wonder. We are changed by its advent; the hard edges of personality are broken. We find new doors set wide in the encompassing walls of our selfhood; the gift of many tongues, new and various possibilities of expression, new instruments of communion with our fellow-men. "And it shall come to pass afterward, that I will pour out My Spirit upon all flesh; and your sons and your daughters shall prophesy, your old men shall dream dreams, your young men shall see visions" - all the splendid possibilities of seer and artist, of the philosopher, musician, and poet, of the revealers of beauty, the deep gazers into things Divine, are included in the Pentecostal gift. His hand sweeps our strings, and evokes new music which we did not dream that we possessed.

But above all it shall sting us to service: to a flaming enthusiasm of ministry, to a declaration and expression of the unsearchable riches of God. His word is with power: it is a dynamic force in those whom it has entinctured, pressing them on to a glad and eager co-operation in the Divine Plan. Part of His mystical body now, they would not be idle members, - "would fain be to the Eternal Goodness what his own hand is to a man." The adult spirit looks upon a new world; yet all about it are its brothers, whose eyes are sealed to the ever-present landscape of Reality. New astounding deeps of experience must be declared to them; and for this, new contacts and mutual understandings must be set up. The arduous communication of the secret of Eternity to each man in a language that he can understand - the language of Science, the language of Beauty, the language of Love - bridges flung out on all sides between the soul of the mystic and other souls of all races, grades, and faiths - universal and exuberant self-donation: this only is the earnest of a life that has attained to its full stature, the mark of man's acceptance as fellow-craftsman with Christ. "I will not leave you comfortless, I will come unto you." Here, through and by the soul that it transfigures, made now the elect vessel of grace, we behold the eternal return, the sudden and generous flowering of the omnipotent Spirit of Love.

Not for nothing did the old painters put our Lady in the very centre of the Pentecostal scene. The soul that has borne God shall spend God. She is the supreme thoroughfare of the Divine Life; and because of the perfection of her union with that life, she receives more abundantly its renewal and its energising fire. Dear, human, and maternal life is here transfigured and made vocative: not merely by the inrush of Divine power and the flooding tide of spirit, but by that greater gift of flaming charity which is the only language of the heart.

Power and charity; the will and the heart blessed to His service, all barriers broken that His Love may pour through us, and be poured out by our human ministry upon all flesh. A universal and fraternal communion is here asked of us: in such a communion the inexpressible gift of His inrushing spirit is first felt. Here, then, is something new in the soul's adventures. Here is forced on it the fusion, not only with God, but with other men in Him: the social experience of Reality, the social act of communion and of prayer. Dependent here as ever on the hard and eager work of the individual will, yet the result which is attained is no merely individual achievement. Of all, through all, in all, the flooding tide of the Eternal Life is felt. *"Orate fratres,"* says the priest at the altar, *"ut meum ac vestrum sacrificium acceptabile fiat apud Deum Patrem omnipotentum."* [15] Set your wills with mine towards the Father; buoy up my little prayer upon your wings. Here is the root of all corporate worship exhibited, and here in this mystery its part in the triumph of life is expressed: the anxious, prayerful, loyal ranks of the Apostles, with the Virgin Mother in the midst; diverse in temperament, diverse in power and vision, yet here welded together in one great instrument, one Body for the Spirit of Christ. Here Mary, who alone on Carmel had been found in her lowliness worthy to be the Mother of her God, humbles herself anew to a dependence on, a co-operation with all those whom that Life which she bore and nurtured has entinctured and redeemed.

Such corporate prayer is in strong souls and pure the highest exercise of charity: in weak souls the glad and humble acceptance of a priceless gift. It is the mark and bond of fraternal love, the bearing of one another's burdens, the perfect fulfilment of the Law of Life. "Alone to the Alone," said the Pagan mystic, and knew than this no closer approximation to the Real. *"Væ soli,"* says the Christian. We seek not the flame of separation. *Accendat in nobis Dominus ignem sui amoris, et flammam æternæ caritatis!* [16] We seek that fire which is the fount of life, the flame of eternal charity; in which, as live coals, "we are burned up by God on the hearth of His infinite love."

Fourth Triumphant Mystery: The Assumption

"*Allons* to that which is endless as it was beginningless" says Whitman. Here is the wayfarer's motto, the rule of the Spiral Road. The homely human life remade, the transient ecstasy of perfect contemplation, even the fertile and inspired career of charity - these cannot content the soul's deepest craving for a perfect fruition of and response to the Beloved. Dante found in the freshness and beauty of the Earthly Paradise no continuing city, but sought at once the Ladder to the Stars; and so it is with every pilgrim of the Infinite who has at last attained the summit of the purging mount of prayer. He too goes up in order that he may "lose himself upon the heights." His newly-anointed senses demand some unalloyed objective; the fire of his all-conquering love demands eternal union with a greater flame. "The souls of the righteous are in the hand of God," and nothing less than this total self-loss in Him can suffice them. He who is here discerned beneath veils, and because discerned, so passionately desired, the mystic would encounter face to face. "Thou hast made us for Thyself and our heart is restless." From Him we came: to Him we must return. Only in His presence is fullness of joy -

> " *Però che il ben, ch'è del volere oblietto*
> *tutto s'accoglie in lei, e fuor di quella*
> *è difettivo ciò che lì è perfetto.*" [17]

Hence it is that the event which common sense had called the "falling asleep" of Mary, our pattern and our mother, that uncommon sense which is the soul's true instinct for Reality has called her "raising up." For indeed, it is less a sleep than an awakening. The emphasis is not upon the laying down to rest of the wearied mind and body at the end of our little busy human day, but rather upon the exultant liberation and uprushing of freed spirit to its home. Men speak of the soul's achievement of this freedom, as of a dreadful rending of that soul from body, the shedding of the essential characters of personality at the bidding of corruption, weakness, death. But it is of the very essence of the story of the Assumption that Mary is here declared to take with her in that last, supremest flight, not some attenuated "spiritual principle" - rather all that we feel most warmly human and most dear.

> *"Transit ad æthera, virgo puerpera, virgula Jesse,*
> *Non sine corpore, sed sine tempore, tendit adesse."* [18]

Humanity in its wholeness is here lifted up into life eternal, into the spiritual Kingdom of the Son of God.

True, that Kingdom is here-and-now, immanent in all things; for heaven, as the mystics tell us, is "a temper not a place," and those who dwell in Christ are there already, though still "entangled in the flesh." In no far land need we seek it; "where the body lies, there is heaven and hell." Yet an assumption there must be, a catching up of created to Creator, not of its own strength and volition, but by surrender to His attractive power, if the soul's cyclic history is to come to its appointed end. Those who have skill to read may find hidden in this mystery the final secret of transcendence; the august declaration of the veritable nature of Man. *Maria Virgo assumpta est ad æthereum thalamum, in quo rex regum stellato sedet solio.* [19] As the nun who kneels before the Tabernacle is caught to communion with a timeless, spaceless Presence, sees the "flaming ramparts" shrink and fade away; so the incarnate genius of humanity entering at last into perfect fruition of the Being of God.

What is that fruition? The mystics try in vain to tell us: for a mighty gulf is fixed between their mind and ours. "Above all knowledge," says Ruysbroeck, of that summit of the soul's transcendence - even the high language of poetry breaking as it were in his hands - "I feel, I discover, I surprise a bottomless and limitless abyss of darkness, that transcends all qualities, that transcends the names of all created things, that transcends the very names of God. Behold! this is that death, that ecstasy of transcendence, that evanishment of all that is most sublime into the One Eternal Mystery, that hoped-for peace which we discern in the deeps of our being, far superior to all external worlds." This is the "Divine Dark" of the great mystics: dim to the earth-trained intellect, most radiant to the heavenward-tending heart. It is the "peace that passeth understanding" of the saints: the dim silence where all lovers lose themselves. Even in our exile we may sometimes look at it, as Plato's prisoners peeping from their cave. But the spirit whose education is finished, who has trod the long way in faith and hope and love, shall come out from this cave to that sunlight "dark with excess of bright" to find that it is no mere Vision, but a Home. That burning prayer of Christ - that all may be one as He and the Father are one, humanity sharing in fact as in name the consummation of its Priest and King - this demands the assumption, the induction of the spirit into that state or region; and receives its perfect demonstration in the "beating Godward" of the humble yet exultant Mother of the Divine Grace. In this act she completes the spiral way which links Divine and human: dying, and behold! she lives indeed.

> ' "At last thou hast departed, and gone to the Unseen;
> 'Tis marvellous by what way thou wentest from the world.
> Thou didst strongly shake thy wings and feathers, and,
> having broken thy cage,
> Didst take to the air and journey towards the world of soul."

She could not help but fly to Him, once the links that bound her to the earth were severed. *Exaltavit humiles.*[20] So little and light she was, so meek and humble, that nothing opposed the steadfast attraction of God. "I was caught up to Thee," said the storm-tossed Augustine, "by Thy Beauty, and dragged back again by my own weight." But the downward pull of selfhood is lifted from the utterly self-naughted soul. "Pure and illuminated," says an old mystic, "she sees nor God nor herself: but God sees this of Him, in her, for her, withouten her; that shows her that there is none but He. Nor she knows but Him, nor she loves but Him, nor she praises but Him, for there is but He." Her weight is her love, and bears her without deflection to the only compelling Centre of the Universe.

In the beautiful old legend of the life and death of Mary, it is said that flowering lilies were found within the tomb where her body had been laid to rest; new life and loveliness upspringing even to the last from the contact of that pure meekness with the world. But the body itself, the tangible witness to them of her presence, those who had loved her found not any more. *Emigravit* ! it was hidden with Christ in God. And Thomas, the careful carpenter, who proved all things by rule and square, looked in the sepulchre and could not believe: for there was nothing on which he could lay hold. The careful dialectic of an intellect apt at the affairs of time and space failed here, and left him in the lurch. Then, says the dear and graceful story, a sign was given him: a sign that the promise of God was true, that Mary lived indeed, and in her all other souls surrendered to His Will. The girdle of her virginity, the zone that circled and fenced in her dedicated life, was let down as it were a link from heaven to earth - witness that its office was fulfilled, since all separations were transcended: that her life was at last become one with the life of the All. "If I embrace Him, I shall be virgin indeed." The primal paradox of fruitful purity is established once more, as in the Annunciation; the flaming secret at the heart of things.

Yet not alone as the uniquely chosen Mother of Christ is Mary made a partaker of the Divine Nature. She is the firstfruits and completion of the Incarnation, the key to all cosmic meanings, an earnest of the perfect indwelling of humanity in God. She goes up, then, as type and harbinger of the race which has struggled in her footsteps up the difficult mountain of self-knowledge and prayer - more, of all creation groaning and travailing even until now, awaiting the transmuting of all things in the Divine image, the perfect manifestation of the liberty of the children of God. The poet sees her thus, going up from the ocean of Becoming; set about with the banners of victory, and bearing in her hands the brimming chalice of intensest life.

> ' "Who is She, in candid vesture,
> Rushing up from out the brine?
> Treading with resilient gesture
> Air, and with that Cup Divine?
> She in us and we in her are
> Beating Godward: all that pine.
> Lo! a wonder and a terror!
> The Sun hath blushed the Sea to wine!
> He the Anteros and Eros,
> She the Bride and Spirit: for
> Now the days of promise near us,
> And the sea shall be no more."

Fifth Triumphant Mystery: The Coronation

The Spiral Way has reached its consummation, and we find that consummation to be one with the great work of the Crucible, as it was conceived by the spiritual alchemists in the past. It is the heavenly work of Love Triumphant: energising love, which is the life of God within the heart. That Mercury of the Wise, the vital principle of growth and change, working in secret, has subdued all things to the measure of its glory: has turned the raw stuff of human nature into alchemic gold. The end of that mystic process, said the hermetic masters, is the raising of the Crowned Queen - Luna, perfected human nature, bride and mirror of the Sun - to a sharing in the splendour of her King. "Lo, behold! I will open to thee a mystery, cries the Adept, the Bridegroom crowneth the Bride of the North." The story of the Coronation of Mary, for them as for us, concealed the mystery of all transcendence. It imaged for them the final consummation of the Spiritual Marriage, the fulfilment of our racial destiny, the utter self-mergence of the soul in the Divine. All other stages of the Way had been but a preparation for this. Here life comes to full circle and highest and lowest, in the bonds of love, are seen to be one thing.

We have followed the soul's life from its first humble act of receptivity, its first simple, eager act of prayer. We have followed the Divine Adventure through the years of natural growth and the years of conscious toil and effort, through weakness and agony, through failure and high triumph - out into the world and back again to the heart of the Living God. Now we see it: the whole cyclic story of the soul accomplished, the crowned Queen of Angels, fellow-partner with the Divine Goodness, enthroned above time and place at the very apex of Reality.

"And the Chanter of Chanters entuned more excellently above all others, saying: Come from Lebanon, my spouse, come from Lebanon, come, thou shalt be crowned. And she said: I come, for in the beginning of the book it is written of me, that I should do Thy will, for my spirit hath joyed in Thee, God of my health."

"For in the beginning of the book it is written of me, that I should do Thy will" - Mary, the humble maiden, perfect thoroughfare of the Divine Idea. Her destiny was fixed in that first willing act of surrender, that opening of her heart to the inflowing Spirit of Life. *Fiat voluntas tua*, and His Will is a remaking of humanity in His image, a fusion of divine and human, of Creator and Created - the union of the Spirit and the Bride. Therein alone the soul discovers her own being; often glimpsed, yet never apprehended, amongst the shifting illusions of earth. In Thy Light shall we see light: in Thy Reality we shall be real. Not of our own strength and power can we ever do it: but by a total appropriation of the heritage stored up for us in Christ.

Of that heritage we have received the earnest-money, in the dowers of grace which helped us on our way. It is His strength within us that has borne us upwards; the starry stranger nesting in our soul. Not in virtue of any private Divine quality, but as the mother of her God, Mary receives the diadem of Everlasting Life. It is His own triumph - the supreme achievement of the Creative Artist wrought within her - that He crowns.

Within that Artist's mind was conceived her image: there it lay hid in its immaculate perfection, "from before the foundations of the world." "Where was I, as myself, as the whole man, the true man?" cries Peer Gynt - poor, hapless wanderer, distracted by many imaginations - in the last, most crucial moment of his life. "Where was I, with God's sigil upon my brow?" And Solveig, who has waited and trusted in defiance of all appearance, replies to him, "In my faith - in my hope - in my love!" It is the voice of the Divine Wisdom that seems here to speak by a woman's lips. There, in His Heart, lies the true being of humanity: defended against all assaults of circumstance by the invulnerable optimism of God.

> *"Thou hast written me in the book of Thy Godhead,*
> *Thou hast depicted me upon Thy Manhood."*

There the image of all that we might be is treasured. Thither we must go, to be conformed to that secret Pattern, if we would find our true selves at last make actual the transcendent personality which every Christian has in Christ. There, in that transfigured humanity, we are gathered up; there, as the beggar maid by Cophetua, we are crowned. We "come to ourselves" indeed: to find in dependence on God the essence of our long-sought liberty and in His eternal service that perfect freedom which belongs only to the prisoners of love. And now we see why it is that His grace can only be upon the humble. *Exaltavit humiles*: for they alone resist not, nor oppose with their cleverness the mysterious operations of the Will. They claim not to do "anything of themselves" and hence are the instruments of His pleasure, the elect vessels of His inflowing Life. When one of these, says Mechthild of Magdeburg, completes her journey and is caught up to God, she can no longer remember the earth and the sorrows of the past. She cares nothing for her glory, nothing for the battles she has won. But she takes the crown from her head, and lays it amongst the roses at His Feet; and asks only one thing, that she may come a little nearer. Then she is taken into the Arms of God; and He looks into her face and embraces her. In that embrace, she is caught to the Highest Height, above all choirs of angels, overpassing in her swift ascent Thrones, Dominations, Powers, her excess of humility transcending in knowledge and in love the very Cherubim and Seraphim who whirl in unending ecstasy about the splendour of the One. The Tree of Life has shot up to the highest heaven, and now at last it bears its flower.

> "*Quivi e la Rosa in the il*
> *Verbo divino Came si fece.*" [21]

As the Communion of Saints is consummated in Mary, so in the Divine Humanity made perfect, the bodily expression of the Word, there is added up all the aspirations and potentialities of the race. They have a part in her victory; within the final flower of her achievement they find their meaning and their rest. She is the Mystic Rose of many petals: all living things that tend to God are gathered in her heart -

> "*Nel giallo della Rosa sempiterna,*
> *che si dilata, digrade, e redole*
> *odor di lode al sol the sempre verna.*" [22]

Within that Mystic Rose, Dante saw Eve, sitting at the feet of Mary healed and made radiant by the reflection of her transfigured countenance. Natural Life, the Mother of Men, in all her strength and splendour, here finds her appointed place. Do what she will, she cannot of her own power come nearer: cannot with her own hand heal the wound of separation that she made. Yet there shall be born of her, and of all to whom her germinal life has been communicated, a Life Transcendent, *umile ed alta più che creatura:* [23] by whose humble receptivity, by whose eager self-donation, her loss may be redeemed. The story of the little girl who ran to God on Carmel, the glad yet timid phrases of self-surrender on her lips, may be read by us as the story of every soul achieving dedication. She is for us the pioneer of creation: the harbinger of an exiled nation going home. She set her feet upon that Spiral Way which links the deeps and heights, the worlds of Becoming and of Being and finds its goal at last in the flaming heart of Reality - Eternal Truth, true Love, and loved Eternity.

FINIS

Footnotes:

Sources and translations of the Latin and Italian passages

1. "If I love Him I shall be chaste,

    If I touch Him I shall be clean,

    If I embrace Him I shall be virgin indeed."

(Roman Breviary: Matins of the Feast of St Agnes: Third Responsary.)

2. Ibid. "O happy mind and blessed soul, that is found worthy to receive Thee, its Lord and God, and in receiving Thee, to be fulfilled with spiritual joy! O how great a Lord it entertains, how dear a Guest brings in, how joyous a Comrade receives, how faithful a Friend does welcome, how lovely and noble a Bridegroom does embrace: even Him who is to be loved before all things that are beloved, and above all things that are to be desired!" (De Imitatione Christi, L. IV., cap. 3.)

3. "O Lord my God, my Creator, and my Redeemer, with such affection, reverence, praise, and honour; with such gratitude, worthiness, and love; with such faith, hope, and purity; do I desire to receive Thee this day, as Thy most Holy Mother, the glorious Virgin Mary, received and desired Thee when to the angel who brought her the glad tidings of the Mystery of the Incarnation she humbly and devoutly replied, Behold the handmaid of the Lord, be it unto me according to thy word." (De Imitatione Christi, L. IV., cap. 17.)

4. "Christ hath flowered in stainless flesh, therefore let human nature rejoice. O human nature, how wert thou dimmed! Thou hadst become like faded grass; but thy Bridegroom hath renewed thee, therefore be not ungrateful to such a lover. This Lover is flower of purity, born in the meadow of virginity; He is the lily of humanity, of sweetness, and of perfect fragrance." (Jacopone da Todi: Lauda C.)

5. "Oh, how great a mystery, how wonderful a sacrament, that the beasts should have seen the newborn Lord, lying in a manger!" (Roman Breviary Matins of Christmas Day: Fourth Responsary.)

6. "To-day Christ is born, to-day the Saviour appears!" (Roman Breviary: Second Vespers of Christmas Day: Antiphon of the Magnificat.)

7. "Compelled not by necessity, but by love."
(De Imitatione Christi, L. III., cap. 18.)

8. "If thou art willing to suffer no opposition, how wilt thou be the friend of Christ?"
(De Imitatione Christi, L. II., cap. i.)

9. "When thou shalt come to this state, that tribulation is sweet to thee, and thou dost relish it for Christ's sake: then think it to be well with thee, for thou hast found Paradise on earth." (Ibid., L. II., cap. 12.)

10. "I fed thee with manna in the desert; and thou hast beaten Me with buffet and scourge." (Roman Missal: Office for Good Friday.)

11. "I gave to thee the royal sceptre: and thou hast given to My head the Crown of Thorns." (Ibid.)

12. "Oh surely needful was the sin of Adam, which was blotted out by the death of Christ! Oh happy fault, which was worthy of such, and of so great a ransom!"
(Roman Missal: Office for Holy Saturday: Exultet.)

13. "Taking also this excellent Chalice into His holy and venerable hands, and giving thanks to Thee, He blessed and gave it to His disciples, saying, "Take, and drink ye all of this. For this is the Chalice of my Blood, the new and eternal testament; the mystery of faith; which shall be shed for you and for many, for the remission of sins. As often as ye do these things, ye shall do them in remembrance of Me." (Roman Missal: Canon of the Mass.)

14. "Wherein are united the earthly and the heavenly; the human and the Divine."
(Roman Missal: Office for Holy Saturday: Exultet.)

15. "Pray, my brethren, that my sacrifice and yours may be acceptable to God the Father Almighty." (Roman Missal: Ordinary of the Mass.)

16. "May the Lord enkindle in us the fire of His love, and the flame of eternal charity." (Ibid.)

17. "For the Good which is the object of the will
    Therein is wholly gathered, and outside it
    That is defective, which therein is perfect."
    (Paradiso, xxxiii. 103.)

18. "The Virgin that childed mounted into heaven, the little rod of Jesse, not without body but without time, she entendeth to be there."
(Caxton's Golden Legend: The Assumption of our Lady.)

19. "Mary Virgin was caught up to the heavenly habitations, where the King of kings sitteth on His starry throne."
(Roman Breviary First Vespers of the Assumption Antiphon.)

20. "He hath exalted the humble." (Luke i. 52.)

21. "There is the Rose, wherein which the Word Divine Made itself flesh." (Paradiso, xxx. 73.)

22. "Within the Gold of the Eternal Rose Which doth expand rank on rank and exhaleth Perfume of praise to the Sun of everlasting spring." (Ibid., xxx. 124.)

23. Ibid. "Lowly and exalted more than any creature."
(Ibid., xxxiii. 2.)

Other works by Evelyn Underhill
from Aziloth Books

Mysticism: unabridged, with original annotated bibliography

Evelyn Underhill was a brilliant scholar who spent many years researching the history and literature of the mystic way. Her book 'Mysticism' was the result of all this endeavour, and has remained the classic in its field, constantly in print since its first publication in 1911. The book is divided into two parts, the first exploring the relationship of mysticism to such diverse subjects as magic, metaphysics, theology and psychology, while Part Two provides a detailed examination of individual mystical consciousness, covering the soul's steps to Illumination. This pioneering study comes with a comprehensive annotated bibliography, allowing present-day students to find the primary texts described with such clarity in Underhill's seminal work.

Practical Mysticism - A Little Book for Normal People

This is a book for the modern-day seeker, a 'How-To' book with a bare-bones description of the techniques that lead to spiritual illumination and poetic insight; a no-nonsense guide shorn of any form of dogma, tradition, sectarianism or appeals to authority. Evelyn Underhill writes with conviction and clarity, leading the reader through such seemingly weighty concepts as contemplation, perception, concentration and surrender of the Self, while leavening the whole with welcome notes of humour and irony. This is an easy book to read and understand, and while the application of its principles may prove harder to accomplish, diligent application of Evelyn Underhill's guidance and advice will unfailingly produce a multitude of blessings.

AZILOTH ||||| BOOKS

Aziloth Books publishes a wide range of titles ranging from hard-to-find esoteric books - Parchment Books - to classic works on fiction, politics and philosophy - Cathedral Classics. Our newest venture is Aziloth Books Children's Classics, with vibrant new covers and Black-and-White/Colour illustrations to complement some of the world's very best children's tales. All our imprints are offered to the reader at a competitive price and through as many mediums and outlets as possible.

We are committed to excellent book production and strive, whenever possible, to add value to our titles with original images, maps and author introductions. With the premium on space in most modern dwellings, we also endeavour - within the limits of good book design - to make our products as slender as possible, allowing more books to be fitted into a given bookshelf area.

We are a small, approachable company and would love to hear any of your comments and suggestions on our plans, products, or indeed on absolutely anything. We look forward to meeting you.

Contact us at: info@azilothbooks.com.

CATHEDRAL CLASSICS hosts an array of classic literature, from erudite ancient tomes to avant-garde, twentieth-century masterpieces, all of which deserve a place in your home. All the world's great novelists are here, Jane Austen, Dickens, Conrad, Arthur Machen and Henry James, brushing shoulders with such disparate luminaries as Sun Tzu, Marcus Aurelius, Kipling, Friedrich Nietzsche, Machiavelli, and Omar Khayam. A small selection is detailed below:

The Prophet	Kahlil Gibran
Herland	Charlotte Gilman
With Her in Ourland	Charlotte Gilman
Frankenstein	Mary Shelley
The Time Machine; The Invisible Man	H. G. Wells
Three Men in a Boat	Jerome K Jerome
The Rubaiyat of Omar Khayyam	Omar Khayyam
A Study in Scarlet	Arthur Conan Doyle
The Picture of Dorian Gray	Oscar Wilde
Flatland	Edwin A. Abbott
The Coming Race	Bulwer Lytton
The Adventures of Sherlock Holmes	Arthur Conan Doyle
The Great God Pan	Arthur Machen
Beyond Good and Evil	Friedrich Nietzsche
The Castle of Otranto	Horace Walpole
Self-Reliance, & Other Essays (series1&2)	Ralph W. Emmerson
The Art of War	Sun Tzu
A Shepherd's Life	W. H. Hudson
The Double	Fyodor Dostoyevsky
The Sorrows of Young Werther	Johann W. Goethe
Leaves of Grass - 1855 edition	Walt Whitman
Analects	Confucius
Beowulf	Anonymous
Plain Tales From The Hills	Rudyard Kipling
The Subjection of Women	John Stuart Mill
The Rights of Man	Thomas Paine
Herland	Charlotte Gilman

Obtainable at all good online and local bookstores.
View Aziloth Books' full list at: www.azilothbooks.com

PARCHMENT BOOKS enshrines the concept of the oneness of all true religious traditions - that "the light shines from many different lanterns". Our list below offers titles from both eastern and western spiritual traditions, including Christian, Judaic, Islamic, Daoist, Hindu and Buddhist mystical texts, as well as books on alchemy, hermeticism, paganism, etc..

By bringing together such spiritual texts, we hope to make esoteric and occult knowledge more readily available to those ready to receive it. We do not publish grimoires or any titles pertaining to the left hand path. Titles include:

Abandonment to Divine Providence	Jean-Pierre de Caussade
Corpus Hermeticum	G.R.S. Mead (trans.)
The Holy Rule of St Benedict	St. Benedict of Nursia
Kundalini	G. S. Arundale
The Way of Perfection	St. Teresa of Avila
Q.B.L.	Frater Achad
The Cloud Upon the Sanctuary	Karl v. Eckhartshausen
The Confession of St Patrick	St. Patrick
The Outline of Sanity	G K Chesterton
The Teachings of Zoroaster	Shapuji A Kapadia
The Dialogue Of St Catherine Of Siena	St. Catherine of Siena
Esoteric Christianity	Annie Besant
The Spiritual Exercises of St. Ignatius	St. Ignatius of Loyola
Dark Night of the Soul	St. John of the Cross
Moses and Monotheism	Sigmund Freud
Man, His True Nature & Ministry	St.-Martin
The Gospel of Thomas	Anonymous
The Imitation of Christ	Thomas à Kempis
The Interior Castle	St. Teresa of Avila
Songs of Innocence & Experience	William Blake
De Rerum Natura	Lucretius
The Secret of the Rosary	St. Louis de Montfort
Tertium Organum	P. D. Ouspensky
De Anima (Concerning the Soul)	Aristotle

Obtainable at all good online and local bookstores.
View Aziloth Books' full list at: www.azilothbooks.com

AZILOTH CHILDREN'S CLASSICS Aziloth Books is passionate about bringing the very best in children's classics fiction to the next generation of book-lovers. Renowned for its original design and outstanding quality, our highly successful list has something to suit every age and interest. Titles include:

The Railway Children	Edith Nesbit
5 Children and It	Edith Nesbit
Anne of Green Gables	Lucy Maud Montgomery
What Katy Did	Susan Coolidge
What Katy Did Next	Susan Coolidge
Puck of Pook's Hill	Rudyard Kipling
The Jungle Books	Rudyard Kipling
Just So Stories	Rudyard Kipling
Alice Through the Looking Glass	Charles Dodgson
*Alice's Adventures in Wonderland**	Charles Dodgson
Black Beauty	Anna Sewell
The War of the Worlds	H. G Wells
The Time Machine	H. G .Wells
*The Song of Hiawatha**	Henry W Longfellow
The Lost World	Sir Arthur Conan Doyle
A Christmas Carol	Charles Dickens
Call of the Wild	Jack London
Greenmantle	John Buchan
Treasure Island	Robert Louis Stevenson
Dr. Jekyll and Mr. Hyde	Robert Louis Stevenson
Gulliver's Travels	Jonathan Swift
Catriona (David Balfour)	Robert Louis Stevenson
The Water Babies	Charles Kingsley
The First Men in the Moon	Jules Verne
The Secret Garden	Frances Hodgson Burnett
A Little Princess	Frances Hodgson Burnett
*Peter Pan**	J. M. Barrie

(* = Full Colour Editions)

Obtainable at all good online and local bookstores.
View Aziloth Books' full list at: www.azilothbooks.com

CPSIA information can be obtained
at www.ICGtesting.com
Printed in the USA
LVOW04s2106211216
518279LV00021B/391/P